Trips around the Great Lakes
Volume One: Lake Erie

David McFadden

The Coach House Press

A Trip around Lake Erie

Toronto *David McFarlane*

Published with the assistance of the Canada Council
and the Ontario Arts Council

ISBN 0-88910-183-3

THIRD PRINTING

Other books by David McFadden:

The Great Canadian Sonnet
(with drawings by Greg Curnoe)

A New Romance

A Trip Around Lake Huron

I Don't Know

On the Road Again

The Poet's Progress

A Knight in Dried Plums

Intense Pleasure

The Ova Yogas

Poems Worth Knowing

Letters from the Earth to the Earth

The Saladmaker

The Poem Poem

Animal Spirits
(with drawings by Greg Curnoe)

My Body was Eaten by Dogs

Canadian Sunset

Gypsy Guitar

A Trip Around Lake Ontario

A Trip around Lake Erie
is dedicated to Ray Woodworth –
painter, sculptor, writer,
union organizer and conservationist –
accidentally shot to death
in Nova Scotia January 3, 1979.

Hamilton, Ontario – on the road map a little blob of yellow at the western tip of Lake Ontario. It's a dirty, dreary, burnt-out industrial city, a place covered by a perpetual black cloud, and it's not considered a great place to live. Yet I love its junkyards, its other-worldly skyline, the mysterious 1920ish architecture of its buildings glimpsed through the swirling clouds of soot.

1

There's Something Magical about Your Place of Birth

My motto has always been Do Nothing Unless It's Absolutely Necessary. I've always had a phobia for absolute passivity and although I think it's made my life more interesting I'll never really know for sure. That's the cutting edge of life: knowing that you'll never know what would have happened if you'd followed the left ventricle of your heart rather than the right and so on. I've often thought about leaving this city but my desire to leave has never been strong enough to overcome the inertia. Actually it's something mystical. There's something magical about your place of birth. But everybody knows that.

There should be a Greek word for overpowering love of birth-place but I can't think of what it might be. Since earliest childhood I've felt that the further you get from Hamilton, Ontario, the less interesting things become, the less magic there is in the air. I can't remember ever being bored in Hamilton but I'm almost always bored outside it. Is it just me or have others had that experience with their place of birth? As if I am bound by a delicate thread, frozen by the utter mysteriousness of my immediate surroundings.

For the past nine years I've been living on the Niagara Escarpment that bisects this city, the same escarpment over which the Niagara River falls forty miles to the east. We live in the shadow of the hospital where I was born, where my wife was born, and where our two children were born.

There is much about the city I hate. The Chamber of Commerce and daily newspaper are Hamilton's Bobbsey Twins. The business community, as in all Canadian cities, is blatantly anti-Canadian and pro-American. But the contempt they display towards their own urban area, the sort of contempt that sees progress in tearing down nineteenth-century mansions to make way for parking lots, is something that no longer exists in most cities of the United States.

But perhaps I'm talking over my head. Such large problems are beyond me. My interests are in the smaller things in life, such as wondering about the magic of your place of birth and how it will magnetize you and immobilize you if you let it and I did.

2
Emily

The great city of Toronto is only an hour's drive but one cannot pretend that one lives there. What one gives to a neighbouring city is something that has been taken away from one's own city, and everyone becomes poorer.

The Canadian painter John Boyle and his wife Janet moved to Hamilton last year during the last few months of Janet's pregnancy so they could be close to the McMaster University Medical Centre. During his time in Hamilton John spent hours walking around the city and loved its strange beauty. With their new baby, Emily, they've returned to their home near Owen Sound. The Canadian poet Christopher Dewdney lived here for six months last year but he's returned to his home-town, London, Ontario. Loneliness is an important part of my life.

3
The View from the Mountain

The incredible European-style series of fountains at Gage Park is still beautiful though fallen to ruin. My series of paintings, Thirty-six Views of the Gage Park Fountains, was shown at the Hamilton Artists' Co-op recently but no one came.

From the Niagara Escarpment, when the view is not obstructed by apartment towers or smog from the steel companies, you can see Hamilton Harbour, the Beach Strip, the Skyway Bridge and the entire west end of Lake Ontario as if it were a huge map. And one can drive all the way up the escarpment, passing through millions of years of rock sediment, and see this view spring to life. I keep thinking of starting my own little tourist bureau, printing up bumper stickers to read WE CLIMBED HAMILTON MOUNTAIN. One often sees bumper stickers reading WE CLIMBED PIKE'S PEAK and certainly Pike's Peak is much taller than Hamilton Mountain. But it probably isn't as steep.

4
The Old Extra-Terrestrial Convention

If someone from another planet were examining the surface of Earth to determine a landing point I'm sure they'd be drawn to the Great Lakes. They're so weird-looking, you just know it must be a key area of the Earth's surface. If there is intelligent life on Earth it would have to be around the Great Lakes.

The little wings of Lake Michigan like a chicken trying to fly, the stubby banana of Lake Ontario, the shark-like fierceness of Lake Superior, the ballet-like grace of Lake Huron and Georgian Bay, the strategically placed points and peninsulas of sad-eyed Lake Erie – all this must tell the thoughtful observer that the Great Lakes were not formed by blind nature. There must be something more to it! Such a vista is so overwhelming it serves to emphasize the insignificance of the individual human being.

And if these extra-terrestrials did decide on the Great Lakes as a landing area I feel they would have to be drawn to the western tip of Lake Ontario: the Hamilton area. It seems such a likely spot on the map, so central to the lakes themselves.

And if there really are extra-terrestrials observing the surface of this planet their name for the Great Lakes would have to be the same as ours: Great Lakes.

5
A Faint Blue Ridge

When I was a kid my parents used to take me to Lake Erie. We had a little cottage there. I remember standing on the beach on a clear day looking at a faint blue ridge on the other side of the lake. I also used to have dreams in which I'd be standing on the beach looking across the lake and the faint blue ridge on the other side would get closer and closer until I'd be able to see trees, buildings, barns, factories, little trucks, trains, cars speeding along the little highways, and sometimes even people. But I never told any-

'Is that faint blue ridge over there?' I asked my dad.

'I don't know,' he said thoughtfully. He was always honest when I asked him questions. 'But I'll ask around for you.'

So he went and asked Ken Featherstone, the old farmer who

rented the land out for the city people to build little cottages.

'Mr. Featherstone says it's the Blue Ridge Mountains of Pennsylvania,' he told me a few days later.

'What is?'

'That faint blue ridge over there that you asked me about?'

'Oh yeah,' I said. 'You know, Dad, I've been thinking that when I'm twenty-one I'm going to buy a brand new 1961 Ford and drive right around this lake.'

6
A Life-Size Map of the Great Lakes

So I decided to write this book. I'd forgotten about my vow to drive around Lake Erie, but now, thirty years later, it became somehow urgent to take my family on this trip. I tried to shake the idea but I couldn't: I had to write a series of five books based on trips around each of the Great Lakes. I vowed to paint a life-size map of each of the Great Lakes with the flaming brush of my crocus-coloured Volkswagen van.

I explained the whole thing to a mercenary friend who writes scripts for movies and television and makes a lot of money. He told me that in order to make the book more saleable I should have someone chasing us. But, like most of the writers I really admire, I don't want to be any richer or any more famous than anyone else. There is simply an urge to have the voice linger on after an imagined death, an urge to make permanent descriptions of what is dying all around us. And I want to be able to take this book with me when I make my next trip around Lake Erie, perhaps twenty years from now. By that time I'll still be writing but 'I' will not in my writing. 'I' will be beyond all that. So this is a farewell of sorts. As is everything.

7
What Lake Should We Go around First?

So on Thursday, June 30, 1977, when Joan said she'd like to go on a short motorcamping trip, I suggested the idea of taking a series of trips around the Great Lakes. She thought it was a good idea. She'd been complaining because she and the kids hadn't been appearing much in my recent writing. She was furious when she read a critical article which said: 'Joan and the kids have been taking a back seat to McFadden's new concerns.' She threw the magazine across the room and said: 'That does it! I knew it all along but it really hurts to see it in print.'

So the timing was right.

Joan had to go to summer school to take an advanced course in special education starting Wednesday, July 6. So we'd have to be home Tuesday night.

'What lake should we go around first?' I said.

'I don't know,' said Joan. 'We don't have much time. Which lake is the smallest?'

It was about three o'clock on the afternoon of July 1, Canada's 110th birthday. If you'd been hitchhiking up the Clappison Cut west of Hamilton, Ontario, about that time you would have seen a canary-coloured Volkswagen van chugging up the hill. The present writer was the driver. Sitting next to him was his wife Joan. His daughters Alison, 13, and Jennifer, 9, were in the back seat along with their dog, Bruce, 3. Earlier we'd dropped the cat off at the boarding kennel.

We had to get some propane for the campstove so we headed up to Courtcliffe Park just off Highway 6 on the way to Guelph. It was the only propane place open on the holiday.

We still didn't know which lake we were going to go around although we had narrowed the choice down to two. It would be either Lake Erie or Lake Huron.

When we got to Courtcliffe Park we paid $5.15 to the girl in the store. She gave us a slip of paper and we took it out back. On top of the store was a forty-foot-tall papier-mâché sculpture of a woman in a bathing suit. We took a picture of her. As I focussed the camera and set up the shot the girl came out of the store to watch. She was laughing. I guess no one had ever stopped to take a picture of this giant Venus de Milo before.

When we drove around the back we found a large green propane tank set on a cement platform which in turn was surrounded by a barbed wire fence six feet tall. On the fence was a yellow sign with blue lettering:

NO SMOKING
within 20 feet
Pro~

I told Joan and the ki
possibility of an explosi
and a bushy Afro hairc
he said with a friendly g

He inserted the hose b
He thought it was alread
it's empty,' I said. 'Why do
he says?'

While he was away I sat on the grass and watched Joan and the kids and Bruce way across the green field. The guy returned a few minutes later – alone.

'Now I know what I was doing wrong,' he said. He gave the hose a twist this time as he inserted it and in a few moments the tank was filled.

The guy's name was Court Belinsky. I guess the park was named partially after him. Anyway he was the grandson of S. Radcliffe Belinsky who runs a massage parlour on the top floor of the Holiday Inn in Hamilton. Radcliffe was a dignified old gentleman who liked wearing expensive three-piece suits. I used to see him going into the hotel every morning. He always walked several paces ahead of his wife. Back a few years when there was a big civic controversy over the tearing down of an old stone armament depot from the War of 1812, Belinsky used to write letters to the editor urging it be torn down. It was in the way of a highway widening project. He said he'd been born in the depot but he wasn't sentimental about it. He never really explained how he came to be born there. Anyway, in a brilliant compromise the city decided neither to tear it down nor leave it standing. They had it moved at a cost of about a million bucks.

It was such a nice day, and it looked as if the park employees were getting ready for a big weekend.

'Anything good going on this weekend?' I asked Court.

'No,' he said. 'Just camping.'

Last year on the July 1 weekend they had a bluegrass festival at the park.

9
Boycott American Culture

One summer a few years earlier we were driving west of Fort Erie along the north shore of Lake Erie on the Canadian side. It was solid private cottage country, with almost no public access to the beaches. Very depressing. All the cottages flew American flags. Joan was really getting browned off.

We drove down a public road to the lake but when we came to the end we saw the beach was all blocked off by private fences. So we had to turn around. There was only one way I could turn and that was by pulling a little way up somebody's driveway.

A woman came running out of her cottage and stood on the verandah screaming at us. There was an American flag flying from her roof.

'Don't you know this is *private property*?' she screamed.

Joan was so steamed she yelled back: 'If you don't like it, lady, why don't you go back where you came from?'

This is kind of strange, because Joan isn't really that nasty a person, nor is she ordinarily anti-American. One of her favourite people in the world is my Aunt Ruth who was born in Buffalo and is a solid US patriot.

Joan later became enthused about the Canadian Liberation Movement which was going strong at that time. So we invited Barry Lord to our place to talk about it. Barry was one of the organizers. He was keeping a pretty high profile in those days. I remembered him from when he went to Delta Secondary School in the east end of Hamilton. I was a couple of years behind him. I remember he used to wear saddle shoes with plaid shoe laces. One year he had a big role in the annual production, *Harvey*. My father went with me to see the show. He was really impressed by Barry. 'That boy is really going to make something of himself,' he said. 'You wait and see.' Being a semi-continentalist and a Pearsonian Liberal, a person who totally distrusts political extremism of all kinds, he now winces whenever I remind him that he said that, which isn't often. I'm not a cruel man.

So Barry sat in an armchair in our front room all night telling us about the Canadian Liberation Movement. Joan was getting impatient. She wanted to know when the Movement was going to start throwing Molotov cocktails through the windows of American cottages on the north shore of Lake Erie.

'The time might come for that but the time isn't ripe yet,' Barry said.

I'd been playing around with the idea of a YANKEE GO HOME bumper sticker campaign and an American Culture Boycott. A total boycott of American movies, American TV, American magazines, American junk food outlets and all that stuff. I was totally convinced it would work, although I found the idea a little frightening at the same time. It takes a special kind of person to get involved in political movements in relatively comfortable times.

Anyway, Barry said the Movement was considering the ideas I brought up. But it never came to anything. He spent a lot of time talking to us that night but we never joined. To me, it was a little frightening, not on a personal level as much as on a national level. To Joan it all seemed just too dull.

Later I heard that the Canadian poet Milton Acorn had left the Movement and nobody knew the whereabouts of Barry Lord. Milton was telling people the Canadian Liberation Movement was totally infiltrated by the Central Intelligence Agency which should have been no surprise to anyone.

'Why don't you denounce them?' somebody was supposed to have asked him.

17

Milton reportedly replied that he didn't want to demoralize the handful of non-CIA members that were still involved.

We were talking about this as we drove up Highway 6 towards the Macdonald-Cartier Freeway, more familiarly known as Highway 401. As we took the ramp onto the west-bound lane of the 401 we made up our mind. We decided to take the counterclockwise route around Lake Erie. From that point on we seemed to enter Magic Time, when every movement of the hand, every breath, every word sends huge waves into the future. My notebook and pen sat on the dashboard in front of me. We felt a little nervous about the whole thing. We were far from the point where one realizes there is no future, there is no past.

10
Art Can Make Boring Things Interesting

Aren't expressways boring? They're the most boring part of any trip. They're so safe they're dangerous. They're about as much fun as eating at McDonald's. After driving west on the 401 for about thirty miles I began to get a little sleepy. We passed a bad accident. One car looked scarcely damaged. The other was on its top. There was clothing and red-stained rags strewn all around. The people had been taken away. It looked bad.

So when we stopped for gas I bought a Coca-Cola and took a few sips. I felt more wide awake immediately. Caffeine has a strong effect on me because I drink so little of it. My heart started beating faster with each sip. It was just like a snort of cocaine. I was alert for the rest of the day.

We drove on the 401 past London where I'd taken Jennifer a few days earlier to drop off the manuscript of my new book, *Animal Spirits,* at Greg Curnoe's studio. Greg was going to draw some pictures for the book. As we arrived the whole Curnoe family was leaving for the show. They were going to see *Star Wars.* So Jenny and I went along with them.

'Did you have any trouble following the plot?' I asked her later. It seemed a little too sophisticated for a nine-year-old.

'No,' she said. 'I understood it perfectly.'

So as we got closer to London Jenny said from the back seat: 'Daddy?'

'Yes?'

'Pretty soon we'll be passing a big sign saying LONDON NEXT FOUR EXITS, right?'

'Right!'

And pretty soon we did.

Driving the 401 has become less boring lately. Seeing Jack Chambers' famous painting of the 401 had a big effect on my way of seeing that expressway. Art can make boring things interesting. When I drive the 401 now one of the things I try to do is find the exact spot where that painting was painted. Last week I was driving along and as I approached London I flicked on the radio and heard that Chambers had died the night before. I later found out his painting of the 401 was a composite rather than one specific view. That was why I had problems finding the spot.

My friend Russell Seaworthy has a Volkswagen van. When he drives along the 401 he sometimes amuses himself by imagining what the van looks like from a point half a mile ahead and a thousand feet in the air.

It's still boring for the kids though. After passing London we took the St. Thomas exit and stopped for a brief rest at Talbotville. We'd go along the lakeshore route the rest of the way. All the way around.

Just before pulling into a gas station in Talbotville we passed a motel with a sign out front reading SPEND A NIGHT NOT A FOR-TUNE. 'That's not bad,' said Joan. 'Just twelve dollars for a single.' She still wasn't crazy about camping.

While Joan and the kids were in the washroom the entire Glenn Miller Orchestra went by in a big bus. GLENN MILLER ORCHESTRA DIRECTED BY JIMMY HENDERSON was painted on the side. Then another bus came by, a church bus. It had on the side BAPTIST BIBLE TEMPLE and on the back A GOING BUS FOR A COMING LORD. The sun was shining. I felt happy I was alive in the twentieth century.

I ran across Highway 4 to a telephone booth, and called a friend in a distant city to discuss some personal matters that are of no interest in the present context. As we talked a beautiful woman got out of a Buick Century with Ohio licence plates and went into the telephone booth next to mine. She started phoning around looking for motel accommodation. She sounded worried. She couldn't find a motel that wasn't all booked up for the night.

11

A Phone Call to an Unnamed Friend

Joan offered to drive for a few hours along Highway 3 and I was happy to let her. She wouldn't want to drive once we crossed the border into the United States of America. It was a beautiful afternoon, a blue sky, no haze, occasional puffy white and grey clouds like an A.Y. Jackson painting.

Highway 3 is the highway that connects Buffalo and Detroit and tends to be a short cut through Canada for a lot of American

12

A Cleveland Radio Station

traffic between those two cities. It's certainly a lot faster than going south of Lake Erie. We rolled along the two-lane, tree-lined road, gradually getting closer and closer to the Lake Erie shore, passing tobacco farms and corn fields and families picking berries and tomatoes. It was so much more pleasant than driving along the angry, mechanical, poisonous Highway 401, and probably safer even though occasional cars whizzed past you the opposite way with only inches to spare.

We passed a water hole with three cows standing thigh deep drinking and a fourth cow walking away as if she'd had enough.

Bruce was lying on the floor. We'd called the Rainbow Bridge in Niagara Falls before leaving home and asked if it would be all right to take him across the border. The guy said we'd need a certificate saying he'd had his rabies shot. We got out his medical certificate and the rabies section wasn't marked off although we knew he'd had his shots so we checked it off ourselves and forged the vet's initials.

As we passed the Chatham Boy Scout Camp I flicked on the radio. We got an FM station from Cleveland just as clearly as if we were on the other side of the lake. It was WDNT FM 108. They played a lot of John Denver songs and stuff like that. I'd heard of John Denver but had never actually been conscious of hearing his songs before. I thought the songs were kind of schmaltzy and full of self-pity. I left the station on though because I didn't want to force my taste on Joan and the kids. They seemed to be enjoying the music although they weren't saying anything. Maybe they disliked it too but didn't want to force their taste on me. After all, I was the one to turn the radio on. And it was my radio. Joan had bought it for me for Christmas.

---

*'A magic is laid
upon land,
upon lake ...'*

13

**Archibald
Lampman**

20

Just past the village of Palmyra we caught sight of grey, shallow Lake Erie, the smallest and shallowest of the Great Lakes, the one that is sick and dying, and, according to scientific prediction, the one that will be the first to disappear, turn to marsh with a thin stream trickling through the middle. But today, viewed from the highway across a mile of low, flat tobacco fields, Lake Erie looked healthy, huge, deep, blue, truly great, and maybe even happy, its choppy waves like white lips trying to kiss the sun to steal a line from Malcolm Lowry, the early Malcolm Lowry that is. If it had been a more honest line I might not have admitted stealing it.

'There's Archibald Lampman', cried Joan.

I looked. Sure enough, there was the cairn commemorating Canada's first postal employee poet. We'd been there last summer and I'd forgotten about it. He was actually buried in Ottawa, the scene of his final series of humiliations where in 1883 he took a job as a clerk in the post office, a job obtained for him by a friend whose father was Canada's postmaster general. Then he began writing a series of sonnets to a fifteen-year-old girl and finally married her. They moved in with his father and mother and three teenaged sisters and quarrelled bitterly. He soon started addressing his sonnets to other women and died at 38 – of a broken heart, it's said!

But here, a mile west of the village of Morpeth, was the peaceful Anglican manse in which he grew up and the church in which his father preached. Dozens of Lampmans are buried in the nineteenth-century cemetery behind the church. Both the church and the cemetery have been maintained much as they must have been in Archibald's childhood. It certainly is a mysterious place, guaranteed to make you feel strangely weepy.

Because Lampman was so much a reflection of this land and this lake he's mine whether I want him or not. It's quite healthy to be schizophrenic in your appreciation of poets who are close to you in time and space. The Canadian poet Dorothy Livesay is far too young to have known Lampman of course – he'd been dead a few years before she was born. But I once asked her what the poets of my generation would have thought of people like Bliss Carman, Charles G.D. Roberts and Raymond Knister, all of whom she knew as a young woman. The Canadian avant-garde of the 1920s. 'I think you would have found them boring', she said. What more is there to say? We had them to feed on.

14
In the Sunny Southland

In Morpeth itself there is a cluster of old brownbrick buildings that must have been around in Lampman's day, must have seen him coming to town on foot or on horseback or horsedrawn wagon or whatever. Hanging out in front of one of the buildings – now used as a variety store – is a spiffy new sign reading ENJOY THE STAR WEEKLY which is kind of strange because that paper folded ten years ago.

There are even fewer clouds in the sky now. The sun is hot on the forehead. It looks as if we're going to miss the hailstorms forecast for the western part of Lakes Erie and Huron tonight. As

Joan drives I open some biscuits and spread cream cheese on them. I wish I had a glass of milk. In the back the kids are screaming at each other. 'Come on, Joan, let's turn around and go home', I say. Suddenly the kids are best friends again.

We pass through Blenheim where the Cadillac Hotel looks like an interesting old place but we don't stop. We pass the Cherry Growers' Co-operative Cold Storage Plant which reminds me we're now entering the sunny southland of Canada, the 'Canadian Tropics'.

15
How I Came to Give up Using the Ampersand

We passed the Cedar Springs/Erie Beach area and the road began skirting the shore. You could watch the road with one eye and the little waves rippling against the sandy shore with the other. There were cars parked at the side of the road and people swimming and sunbathing.

We were still listening to the Cleveland radio station when we passed a fruit farm with a sign reading ROBERT CLEVELAND & SONS. An ampersand! My mind went back to Winnipeg where I'd been playing the role of the Visiting Poet a few months earlier. A neurotic high school teacher was reprimanding me for using ampersands in my writing.

'Why can't you use "and" like everyone else?' she kept saying.

'I like the various shapes of the ampersand in the various type styles', I said. But she wasn't listening.

'I just can't understand why your writing is so full of ampersands'.

'It's a tribute', I said, 'to my favourite poet William Blake who always used them'.

'I just can't understand why your writing is so full of ampersands', she said, as if for the first time. I was beginning to realize there was something the matter with her but compassion was setting in.

'Look lady', I said. 'If it'll make you feel any better I hereby vow and you're my witness that I'll never use an ampersand again as long as I live'. I looked at her. She had that funny look in her eye. I realized she hadn't heard me.

'Irving Layton never uses ampersands', she said.

She had a tremendously pained expression on her face as if she were having trouble breathing. Each time I spoke you could tell she couldn't hear me because she was too busy thinking about how much she hated me and how unfair it was that I got my poems published but she couldn't.

Sure enough, someone later told me she was asthmatic, suffered from migraines, wrote sonnets, and had a broken-down drunk for a husband.

I wasn't about to knock on the door and ask Robert Cleveland or his sons but I bet no one ever gave them heck for using an ampersand on that sign. Further, I bet they were direct descendants of Moses Cleveland, the seventeenth-century Englishman who came to the US and founded the city of Cleveland just across the lake.

Moses Cleveland was a contemporary of the English poet John Cleveland and was the great-grandfather of Grover Cleveland, a US president and one-time mayor of Buffalo in the nineteenth century.

I don't think I ever met anyone named Cleveland. Have you?

It's certainly not an obsolete name though. There's only one Cleveland in the Hamilton phone book, an S.R. Cleveland, but there are twenty-eight Clevelands in the Toronto phone book, not counting Cleveland Controls, Cleveland Tramrails, Cleveland Trencher Division, Cleveland Twist Drill Canada Ltd., and Cleveland House.

Cecil Cleveland lives at 20 Tinder Crescent in Toronto and his phone number is 755-7855.

Bill Cleveland is dean of arts at Simon Fraser University.

I would mention Reggie Cleveland, the major-league pitcher who once beat the Cleveland Indians, but I don't know anything about baseball.

16

Beyond the Blue Horizon

No matter how fast Joan drove, the lake was still there and would be for days. Lake Erie was blue and choppy. At certain places the water was blue all the way from the horizon to the shore. At other spots it developed layers of colour like an exotic drink: a yellow band close to the shore, a green band further out and a blue band stretching out to the horizon, corresponding to the various depths I suppose.

We passed some small peach orchards. There are only three places I know of in Canada where peaches can be grown: the Okanagan Valley, the Niagara Peninsula, and here. Soft fruit country. Like Georgia.

I didn't know what the kids were doing but they were quiet. I was looking past Joan at the water. Joan probably thought I was looking at her. She was looking straight ahead at the unwinding road. 'I'm okay, aren't I?' she said. She must have been having a moment of existential doubt, a rare thing with Joan as she is basically highly secure. Like the Royal Canadian Mint.

'Okay about what?'

'About everything.'

'Yeah. I guess so. Sure you are.'

'We've come through a lot together, haven't we?'

'Yeah. We sure have. I was just thinking that.' There must have been something in the air. I'd heard an interview with Gore Vidal on the radio a day or two before. He was saying that whenever he hears the word 'love' he checks his wallet. There is only lust, he said, and there can be no lust between two people who have been living together any length of time. Just then I began feeling a wave of love towards this woman whom I'd been living with for so many years I've lost count. But then again, Gore, maybe I didn't feel it. Maybe I just thought I did. You better check your wallet.

Then on the western horizon I noticed something. At first I thought it was the faint distant skyline of a large city – maybe Detroit. But no of course it couldn't be Detroit yet. I refocussed my eyes and the faint line became not the tops of buildings but the tops of trees.

'There's Point Pelee,' I said.

'Where?' said Joan.

'Over there! Look!'

The kids were stirring. 'Are we going to Point Pelee?' said Jenny.

'Yes we are,' said Joan. 'And we're going to take the ferry to Pelee Island and then across to the United States.'

'Tonight?' said Jenny, trying to disguise her excitement.

'I don't know,' said Joan. 'We're not going on the ferry tonight, are we Dave?'

'No. Tomorrow morning.'

17

The Ketchup Drips All Over the Chips

As we approached the town of Wheatley, Joan wanted me to decide whether we'd camp at Wheatley Provincial Park for the night or head down into Point Pelee and try to locate Russell Seaworthy. It occurred to me that maybe Russell wouldn't want to see us but after some hesitation I said, 'Let's go to Point Pelee.'

'He might be on a field trip,' warned Joan.

But as we passed Wheatley Provincial Park Joan said, 'Oh, look! All the campsites are filled. No vacancies. I bet we're going to have trouble getting campsites all the way around Lake Erie.' After all, this was a special long weekend both for Americans and Canadians: Friday, Saturday and Sunday for Canadians and Saturday, Sunday and Monday for Americans.

Point Pelee juts down into Lake Erie in much the same way

that Prince Edward County juts down into Lake Ontario. The two towns at the top of Point Pelee are Leamington and Wheatley. The two corresponding towns at the north end of Prince Edward County are Belleville and Trenton. Prince Edward County is a much larger peninsula than Point Pelee, and likewise Belleville and Trenton are much larger towns than Leamington and Wheatley. Highway 3 runs through Leamington and Wheatley while Highway 2 runs through Belleville and Trenton. And Highway 2 continues across the immensity of Southwestern Ontario before meeting Highway 3 just outside Windsor. Windsor is the centre of a clock – with one hand, Highway 2, pointing at Montreal, and the other hand, Highway 3, pointing at Buffalo.

Al Purdy is the poet of Prince Edward County. Russell Seaworthy is the poet of Point Pelee.

Past Wheatley we noticed that the corn looked a lot further along than it had forty miles back, but it also looked as if there'd been an awful storm. There was too much water lying in the fields and branches had been knocked off trees and were lying around. When we approached Leamington we saw a huge tall old birch which had been completely uprooted in front of a stately old home. The tree had probably been there since the home was built. And now it was finished. Never to be replaced.

Joan was following the green signs indicating the route to Point Pelee. We turned left at the main intersection and started heading south. We passed the familiar old Heinz plant which straddles the road. A sign in front said NO TOURS.

'Hey kids, that's where they make ketchup,' said Joan.

'Heinz Ketchup,' I added, for no special reason.

'Hey,' said Jenny. 'I've been here before.'

I started singing part of Stompin' Tom Connors' song about Leamington:

> *They romp and run around Leamington*
> *And boy when they get hungry*
> *The ketchup drips all over the chips*
> *Way down in tomato country.*

18

Dropping in on D.H. Lawrence

At the entrance to Point Pelee National Park is a small gatehouse where a self-important woman checks people entering and leaving. She looked up at me as if I were a criminal. She flipped through a couple of sheets of paper on a clipboard and said she knew of no Russell Seaworthy renting a cottage within the park. I could hear the kids cracking peanuts in the back of the van. 'It's not allowed, you know,' she said. At first I thought she meant

25

eating peanuts. Then I realized she meant staying in the park overnight.

'Perhaps you've seen his van?' I said. 'It's a bright red Volkswagen.'

'No,' she said sternly. She wanted me to know that she didn't want to hear any more about it. She was above that kind of public relations work. She took my two dollar entry fee. It was almost dark. She obviously thought there was something suspicious about someone entering the park so late in the day and was a little annoyed that there was nothing she could do about it except to say what she did say. 'There's no overnight camping,' she said.

'Yes, I know,' I said, politely. I was trying to be as polite as Russell Seaworthy would be under these circumstances. 'We'll just look for our friend and if we can't find him we'll leave.'

We drove about two miles into the park before seeing Russell's van. We pulled up beside it. Russell came out on the verandah of a nice freshly painted cottage. The cottage looked as if it had been built around 1936. Russell was bathed in the golden light of early evening. He was dressed in a blue shirt and a pair of white drawstring pants. He was barefoot and very tanned. He looked wonderful.

'The McFaddens!' he said. 'You're the last people I expected to see here.'

Diane came out behind him. She said she had been quite ill with a lung infection for the past two weeks. In fact she came to join Russell at Point Pelee simply to try to shake the stubborn infection. Perhaps the hot sun and clear skies might do the trick. Her daughter Junie stood beside her stark naked as usual. The first time I saw Junie she was fully dressed and for some reason I said to her: 'Why don't you take off all your clothes and jump up on my lap and we'll hug and kiss and stuff like that?' Expecting her to say no sir, not on your life. But she did, which was kind of embarrassing. Latency periods seem to be going the way of the passenger pigeon.

Russell said he'd been cycling, hiking, birdwatching, swimming, sunbathing, and reading Wyndham Lewis novels since arriving at Point Pelee. He'd been doing a lot of painting in water colours, acrylics and pencil crayons. And he'd been doing a lot of late-night writing on a small portable typewriter at the kitchen table. Altogether he'd written seventy pages on his science fiction novel and about twelve pages of a long poem. I kept glancing at an old bus that had been wheeled into a space next to the cottage maybe thirty years before and simply left there. It looked as if it had been a church bus at one time. The wheels had been removed.

It was sitting at the side of the cottage and first had been used as extra living quarters. Later it had been used strictly for storage. Now it was just mouldering away, the evening sun slanting through its dirty, paint-smeared windows. It looked as if it might have been the British Columbia painter Emily Carr's caravan from the 1930s.

I was swamped by déjà-vu after déjà-vu. It was as if I'd decided against visiting Russell at Point Pelee on this trip. And now I was an old man, looking back over my life and bitterly regretting not having paid Russell that visit. I was imagining what it would have been like. Isn't that strange? It struck me as being totally strange, a very eerie feeling as befits someone on a trip around Lake *Erie*. I had to reach out and touch Russell to make sure he was really there, and it was really only 1977.

And then the strangeness transformed itself. It was as if we had gone back in time and were visiting D.H. Lawrence. The sun seemed to have reversed itself. You could see *Kangaroo* on the typewriter.

'Now we've got someone to challenge at Scrabble', said Diane who looked a little grey.

'Are you on medication?' said Joan.

'Oh, I've got bottles and bottles of pills'.

We were standing inside the cottage. It was really a comfortable place. There were partitions dividing it into a living room, with a bedroom at the rear, and a kitchen with a washroom at the front and another bedroom at the rear. The furnishings were all circa 1940: lamps, armchairs, bed-chesterfields, kitchen tables and chairs in painted wood.

'We'll have to rent it next year', said Joan. As I said before she's really not crazy about camping. Neither am I. I don't know why we do it.

'Sure', said Diane.

Just then Bruce puked on the floor. He stood there looking kind of stupid, an orange pool of guck on the floor at his feet, just inside the front door. What an intrusion on such a peaceful scene! I wish we hadn't bothered them at all.

I grabbed a rag and cleaned up the mess. Joan patted him, saying, 'Ah, Brucie, poor doggy, poor Brucie-Wucie'. I thought he'd been eating peanuts in the shell although there weren't any shells in the vomit and peanuts aren't orange.

'Maybe he's caught what Diane's got', said Joan, in her own inimitable brand of humour.

19

Bruce Pukes on the Floor of Russell Seaworthy's Cottage

'So soon?' said Diane.

20

The Collingwood Poetry Festival

'I feel strange' I confided to Russell, 'as if we're time travelling, visiting some writer from the past like Charles G.D. Roberts or Raymond Knister' I didn't want to say D.H. Lawrence, because Lawrence wasn't Canadian and it might have sounded a little pretentious. Besides I don't think Russell had ever been interested in Lawrence. It was totally my own projection.

'God', said Russell, 'I hope it's someone better than Charles G.D. Roberts or Raymond Knister'

For a moment there I'd forgotten how highly Russell regarded himself as a writer. He's such a humble person up front it's easy to disregard the highly structured ego at the back of his brain. His dedication is incredible, all the more so when you think of how his three published books have been ignored by all but a few.

A month or two earlier he had been birdwatching in the Collingwood area. He was listening to the radio in the van and found out that there was a poetry festival going on in Collingwood, with big name poets – if that's not a contradiction in terms – from all over Canada in attendance. You know, the ones who get interviewed by Robert Fulford on television and on Sunday morning arts programs and CBC radio. The ones who are easily understood because they keep reworking and rewriting the same poem and deal with one very limited, highly monotonous and easily recognizable theme.

'It sounded just dreadful', said Russell. 'The interviewer was chasing Joe Rosenblatt around because he'd just won the Governor General's Award. She asked him what he did when young poets show him their work. He said, "Oh, if they have any talent at all I'll spend a few minutes with them. Otherwise it's boring."'

'Do you wish you'd been there?'

'Oh I was glad I wasn't there. That's for sure. But it sort of irked me, I must admit, that I hadn't been invited'

21

The Seacliffe Hotel

Russell and I left the women and girls at the cottage and drove off in his van. We were going to the Seacliffe Hotel to check the ferry schedule for the following day.

Back at the gatehouse we asked the same self-important woman if she had a ferry schedule. The asphalt road looked for a moment as if it were on fire. I looked again. It was just the reflection of the setting sun through a curtain of poplars.

I half-expected the woman to say, 'Oh, a bright red Volkswagen

28

van. Someone is looking for you! But no, oh no! Not her. She just looked at us characteristically as if we were criminals. Maybe she always looked like that and it was really no indication of her mental state. Maybe she was born looking like that, or born to look like that. Needless to say she had no schedule and didn't offer any ideas where we could get one.

We went through the park exit and onto the highway. I took the opportunity to extend a sincere apology to Russell for having missed his poetry reading in Toronto a while back. I hadn't found out about it until it was too late. However, aside from me, the small band of Seaworthy aficionados was out in force. Greg Curnoe had been there and said it was a good reading. 'Russell's a real comic, you know,' he said. 'He knows exactly how to play an audience. He was reading these poems about sharp objects falling from the sky and people picking them up and cutting themselves. What a funny guy!'

Russell accepted my apology gracefully. Then he began telling me about seeing a legless hitchhiker on the side of the highway as he drove down to Point Pelee. I think this was his way of paying me back for missing his reading, punishing me when I perhaps seemed to be most asking for it.

'He was lying on the ground pointing his crutch at the passing cars,' he said.

'Did you stop for him?' I knew he hadn't.

'No. But if you'd been in the van I would have. You could have written his life story in a poem.' So it had come to this, had it? Less than two years ago Russell had come to me expressing intense admiration for my writing and now he was making fun of me. I suppose I'd asked for it. There always seemed to be a certain sense of cruelty in Russell. You could see it occasionally in his writing also.

Then as we drove along I told Russell I was planning to write a short documentary novel called *A Trip around Lake Erie*. He seemed to like the idea. So then I told him I wanted to write a similar book for each of the Great Lakes, a five-book series. There was just a slight hesitation, my animal instincts telling me he was briefly wondering if I were trespassing on his territory. But no, that's ridiculous, he seemed to be thinking, I can't stake claims to the entire Great Lakes.

'Sounds like a *great* idea,' he said, beaming with enthusiasm.

As we entered the hotel we stepped over the date of construction, 1938, inlaid in a kind of mosaic pattern in the floor just inside the front door. I'd just been wondering when it was built. It was a three-storey brick structure with an interesting pattern of **29** first-floor lounges and dining rooms. A little like Hartley House in Walkerton but smaller. We walked through a hallway and into a lounge with a four-foot-high television screen showing a baseball game in progress. At the other end of the lounge an outmoded three-piece rock group was performing along with an overly amplified female singer. There were about a dozen people in assorted small groups ignoring both the television and, with much more difficulty, the band. Some of the windows were open and the special atmosphere of Lake Erie was filtering in, a grey mysteriousness that seemed to be funnelling out of an earlier part of the twentieth century.

We walked past a large horseshoe-shaped bar behind which a fat woman in her forties was reading the *TV Guide,* and entered another lounge with pool tables and pinball machines and less comfortable tables and chairs.

Another fat woman about twenty-four years old and boasting a withered arm was energetically playing one of the pinball machines. There were quite a few fat people around. There were several fat and surly men in their twenties looking as if they would become violent if they caught you looking at them.

'Hey, whaddaya think you're lookin' at, eh?'

I looked away.

'It's kind of rednecky around here,' said Russell. He'd spent a few evenings here during the ten days or so he was at the cottage before Diane and Junie arrived.

There was a public telephone behind the pinball machine and I made a few phone calls trying to get ahold of someone in charge of the ferry docks at Leamington, Kingsville, Pelee Island, or even Sandusky, Ohio. But there were no answers to any of the numbers.

22
Russell Dines Out with Some Biologists

'There are some biologists drinking in the other room,' said Russell. 'They'd probably know the schedules.'

We went into the other room. Russell introduced me to two women and three men relaxing after a hard day answering tourists' questions at the Point Pelee Nature Interpretive Centre.

We were sandwiched between the huge television screen where someone had just hit a pop fly and the bandstand where the singer's breasts seemed about to pop out. My eardrums were screaming.

Russell asked about the schedules but I couldn't hear their answers. They were looking at me and moving their lips and I just smiled back.

I figured out this much: the biologists were going to drive to Windsor as soon as they finished their beer. There was going to be a big Canada Day fireworks display. They wanted us to come along with them, at least the two women did.

It turned out a ferry was to leave at nine in the morning but no one knew whether it left from Leamington or Kingsville. They knew it stopped at Pelee Island but they didn't know how long it stayed there before going on to Sandusky.

We went back into the other room where the pinball machines and pool tables were located. We ordered beer.

One of the women biologists came over to our table. 'Are you sure you can't come to Windsor with us?' she said. She was lovely.

'Afraid we can't tonight,' said Russell.

After she went Russell said the biologists had really been nice to him throughout his stay, patiently answering all his complex questions about the natural history of the area, and they even took him out to dinner at the Seacliffe Hotel one memorable night.

'I didn't say a word throughout the whole meal,' said Russell with a gentle laugh. 'I felt totally out of place.'

'I guess they weren't talking about the natural history of Point Pelee?'

'Oh, no. They were just talking about university and various people they knew. I don't know what they must think of me.'

'They probably just think you're quiet,' I said. 'And probably very romantic.' I remembered that Russell doesn't eat meat. 'What did you have?'

'Fresh Lake Erie perch fillets.'

'Hmm ... Yum, yum!'

'I'd love to be able to go back in time and see this hotel as it was in the late 1930s and 1940s.'

'Yeah,' said Russell. 'That would be great.'

In the van Russell began speaking of his writing. I knew he'd eventually get around to it. He went on and on talking about the transforming effect his writing was having on his personality, and the difficulty he is having getting his characters to obey his orders.

'The novel is being written in the third person so there's no earthly reason why the main character can't simply ride away from the action,' he said. I think he was hoping I'd give him some magic word that would solve the riddle.

'But you don't want to *force* him out of there,' I said.

23

On Being Fascinated with What Is Going on around You

'That's right. Come to think of it, I suppose he is so fascinated with what is going on around him that I don't want to do anything that will interfere with that fascination.'

24
Full Moon over Point Pelee

As we drove through the early night the trees parted and there it was: a full moon rising over Point Pelee. The waves on the west shore were smashing into the breakwater rocks and exploding into the air, each drop reflecting a miniature moon, millions of miniature moons.

Russell agreed that each of the lakes has a totally different character. He said Lake Erie was melancholy, gloomy, misty. I said I expected Lake Erie to have the same atmosphere all the way around and I was anxious to find out. We agreed that Lake Erie is our favourite lake. I told him I simply didn't want to live my entire life without having travelled completely around each of the lakes. It just had to be done.

Of course at the same time I realized the whole notion was completely ridiculous. What a silly ambition! It would be more sensible to try to become a millionaire or something like that. The world often seems an unfit place for people of modest ambition. You have to be a bit of a killer before anyone will respect you. So who needs respect?

But the Great Lakes are an important part of my life. I'm conscious of being surrounded by them. The writing was a way of justifying the trips, a way of making them seem suitably important. But it was also a way of giving evidence of these feelings at this point in the planet's history. That this is one of the ways consciousness felt about these lakes in the twentieth century, if that doesn't sound too pretentious.

25
The Moose Population of Quebec

Again the woman at the gatehouse looked at us as if we should be arrested and held without bail. Two men in a van entering a national park this late at night? They must be degenerates of some sort. Of course Russell's van was quite distinctive in appearance. But she didn't want to let on she recognized him and knew he had rented a cabin in the park. No overnight camping was allowed and since the park had been established no new cabins had been allowed to be built. The government had bought up all the cabins they could. And although the government policy fell short of outright expropriation, they had a million ways of letting cottagers know they weren't wanted.

This was one of the ways. This woman had somehow absorbed

the unspoken attitude existing between the lines of official policy. Another form of human corruption, the same process no matter what the system. A human being will not hesitate to make another human being feel uncomfortable if there is any advantage at all to be gained. I'll never forget the car wash attendant in Brunswick, Georgia, who glared hatefully at me for an astounding three seconds because I hadn't put on my brakes at the precise moment he dropped his hand. I could just imagine squadrons of goons like him breaking into tiny Vietnamese villages and hacking away at the men, women and children. But we're supposed to forget all that now.

At least she wasn't armed. The Point Pelee woman, that is. A while back I was driving down to Montreal from the north of Quebec and had to pass through La Verendrye National Park. The guard had a huge revolver in a holster strapped to his waist.

'What's with the gun?' I said.

He said something in French I didn't catch.

I pointed to his gun. 'Has Quebec joined the United States already?'

I could tell by his eyes he understood perfectly. But he tried to pretend he didn't.

He handed me a bilingual leaflet warning drivers to beware of moose on the road.

It said, in part: 'Not only can a collision with a moose result in damage to the car and perhaps serious injury to the motorist and passengers, it is also not very beneficial to the moose population of Quebec.'

But the eyes of the woman at the Point Pelee gatehouse were incredibly evil. She said nothing but looked as if she *knew* what unspeakable crimes we were in the habit of committing.

'You'd think she'd recognize me by now,' said Russell, mildly.

26
Playing Games

Back at the cottage we ate sandwiches and peanuts and played Scrabble. It wasn't a very exciting game. The words didn't come right for any of us. I kept having the feeling we were intruding, although Diane and Russell were most hospitable. Yet with Diane's illness, she obviously would have been more comfortable without the McFadden family around. And of course Russell would probably be writing right now if we hadn't arrived not only unannounced but uninvited.

Russell kept getting Point Pelee words such as BIRCH and DUNE. That was sort of interesting. Joan went out first, but Diane won as far as points were concerned. Diane scored 117, Joan 96, and Russell and I tied with 105 each. Funny, the last time we'd bowled together we tied too. At this point in the story I wanted to record every detail of the game and go into it with a detailed commentary, even though the game wouldn't be as worth recording, say, as the Go games in Kawabata's *The Master of Go*. I have the complete record of the game right here next to my typewriter. But no, I don't think I'll bother.

Recently I was talking to Russell on the phone and reminded him of our Point Pelee Scrabble game. 'Oh yeah, that was a good game', he said brightly, after I read him the list of the words he'd used. 'That was a great visit', he said. 'I'm going to be up there in June and July and you're welcome to come whenever you want.'

27
Seeing Canada Vanish under the Waves

After the game, Diane began stretching and yawning. Soon Russell and I were the only ones up. Russell got out his typewriter and set it up at the kitchen table where we'd been playing Scrabble. In spite of the visitors and Diane's illness Russell seemed to be at some kind of spiritual peak. You could see him quietly smouldering, and occasionally bursting into brilliant flame. The stay at Point Pelee was obviously doing him a lot of good. You could see little Point Pelees in his eyes.

'It's really beautiful on nights when there is no moon', he said. 'I take a flashlight and get on my bicycle and ride down to the point. The whole peninsula is totally black. It's a spooky experience.'

I'd been to the point once, and that had been a year ago. Yet even then, in full daylight, there was something decidedly mysterious about it. You know exactly where you are geographically, right at the southernmost tip of Canada, and it is a very *clear* experience somehow. You just know you're standing at some kind of significant point although that doesn't make any kind of pragmatic sense. You can see the point continue on under the water, and you can see the waves from the west meet the waves from the east at the place where the land would be if the water level were lower. The biologists stationed in the park say the point over the years keeps swinging back and forth through the water. It's like a dog's tail, they say. It never stops wagging. But the motion is too slow to see.

When I was there it was a hot summer afternoon and tourists were taking turns walking out to the point then wading further out to the narrow sandbar and having their pictures taken at Canada's southernmost point. Being there was one of those rare *Canadian* experiences, like watching a lacrosse game between

Six Nations and Owen Sound at the Brantford Arena, or finding copies of Fred Cogswell's Fiddlehead books in the bookstore in Yellowknife. The painter Greg Curnoe once mailed a postcard from Pelee Island to Alert, from the southernmost Canadian post office to the northernmost.

Anyway, it really is fun to have your picture taken smiling, pants rolled up, wading off the point of Point Pelee, even though the camera may catch a small island sitting there mindlessly on the horizon. That's Pelee Island, also part of Canada, and even further south. But that doesn't really count. It's the southernmost part of *mainland* Canada that is the magical point.

And the Americans of course don't bother walking to the point. They just lie on the beach in their bathing suits, drinking beer and cooking hotdogs. Grumbling about Communism and Ralph Nader. I heard one of them say: 'We're smarter than the Russians. We got a man on the moon.'

'I've got about two hours worth of work to do,' said Russell as he started typing. Someday you might read this novel and remember having read this story in which part of that novel was written. The working title is *Planet of Heavenly Peace*. Strange that both 'heaven' and 'heavy' would have similar Old English roots.

28
Dog-Eating Dragons

It was a warm summer's night and I decided to take Bruce for a walk. We walked south on the road banked by poplar trees sixty feet tall. The full moon was low in the southern sky, and the road appeared to be heading right into it. Everything was warm silver and voluptuous black. There were no street lights of course, no traffic lights, no lights from all-night restaurants, not the slightest whisper of traffic in the distance. Just the odd cottage with a slight candle glimmering in through the trees like a low-lying star.

Slight wind currents made the tall trees crack occasionally like cracking knuckles.

I was certain I wouldn't want to bicycle all the way to the point with a flashlight on a moonless night. Russell was right. It would be spooky.

We walked about two miles, Bruce giving low barks whenever a tree would crack its knuckles. I heard a good definition of the word bark: 'The outer sheath of trees and dogs.'

Point Pelee is on a major North American flyway but there didn't seem to be any nocturnal birds around, at least no noisy ones. Bruce kept close to me. He seemed aware of being in extraordinary circumstances and he was a little cautious. He probably thought we were approaching the gates of hell. I really couldn't tell if he was staying close to me because he wanted to protect me or because he wanted me to protect him.

For me, it was just like a return to the nineteenth century. An average narrow country road in Ontario at night. Something out of *Wacousta*. There was something about the atmosphere of the place that made the notion of chucking civilization even more attractive. Just coming out of the woods on dark nights to smash the windows of McDonald's hamburg places or slash the tires of municipal politicians. Oh, what a wonderful life!

As for Bruce, I guess he was expecting to be attacked by man-eating dragons at any moment — or rather dog-eating dragons. As an experiment I made a slight hissing sound. Bruce froze, his ears fully erect.

29
The First Mention of Dead Fish

In the morning Bruce and I were awake before anyone else so we ran over the dunes and down to the west beach.

Out there on the horizon, as it has for a thousand years, sat Pelee Island, a fringe of dark blue-grey between the light blue-grey sky and the green-grey lake. It's about fifteen miles and takes ninety minutes to get there by ferry from Seacliffe or Kingsville. I sat in the sand and watched a couple of fishing boats inching along the horizon.

I kicked off my sandals and ran along the beach, careful to avoid stepping on the dead fish. Bruce ran in front of me, occasionally looking back over his shoulder. His tongue was hanging out as if he had swallowed a bright red tie.

The sand became too soft, my feet going down four or five inches with each step. It became too difficult to run and I began slowing down. Then I couldn't run anymore. I fell to my knees. Bruce stopped running and cocked his head at me as if to say, 'What's wrong?'

There was quite a breeze and the breeze was churning the waves. There were thick whitecaps all the way out to the horizon, appearing, moving in like low-flying gulls, then disappearing. There was a feeling of being in the sub-tropics, the Canadian sub-tropical zone, with the vegetation as lush as a tropical rain-forest — vines curling up the trunks of small trees and Spanish moss hanging from tall branches like the dry unkempt beards of old hermits.

I performed my regular morning exercises in the sand with the wind on my back and in my hair. It felt wonderful. Then I remembered that last night, when Russell and I were at the hotel, Joan had taken the dog down to the beach. Joan told me that all the time he was down there he kept rolling on top of the dead and rotting fish that dotted the shoreline. He became so smelly that Joan had to bathe him.

So I looked and sure enough he was doing it again. How stupid of me! Joan would kill me. He was rolling over and over back and forth on every dead fish he came to.

And then he would stand there and piss on each one. And then roll over it again.

I quickly brought him back up to the cottage. It was kind of sad. I'd have liked to have joined Bruce in pissing on the fish and rolling over and over on them.

30
A Skeleton in the Trust Company

Then the sun came up over the giant poplar trees surrounding the sad little cottage and we ate a hearty breakfast and took dozens of photos of each other with Russell's camera. Then we said good-bye, see you in time, in Hamilton, in Toronto, somewhere, and drove off.

In Leamington I parked the car and went into a trust company to buy some US money. The whole town was flooded with the most intense sunlight but it was cool and shady inside. It was Saturday and there were only two women working, no customers. Here I made the kind of faux-pas anyone could make.

'Skeleton staff today?' I said to the women, innocently trying to make a cheerful joke. As I said it I sucked my cheeks in and opened my eyes wide to try to look like a skeleton.

Neither woman laughed. Then I noticed that one of them did indeed look like a skeleton – sunken eyes, drawn face, extremely thin arms and legs. She looked a hare's breath from death. They doubtlessly thought that I had made some extremely thoughtless and cruel joke, and there was no way I could apologize without making the whole thing worse.

Can you imagine me trying to apologize? What would I say: 'Oh, I'm sorry. I had no idea that you looked like a ... Well, I just said that as a joke before really looking at you ...' It just wouldn't work.

Of course thin people are often more sensitive about their appearance than the obese. One woman I know always bursts into tears whenever anyone draws attention to her thinness. Yet the thinnest person I know, a Jewish poet who is obsessed with concentration camps, takes great pride in his emaciated body. In fact he puts saccharine in his coffee and refuses to eat bread and pastries. That I can truly understand though. I think most of us would be a lot happier and less neurotic if we cut our food consumption by 90 per cent.

The thin woman waited on me. It cost me $106.65 in Canadian money to buy $100.00 in US funds. She gave me five funny-looking twenties with pictures of some guy in a nineteenth-century beard.

Just to remind you: this was the summer of 1977, just a few months before it became totally obvious to everyone that Canada was heading inevitably for total union with the United States.

I looked at the woman again just before I pocketed the money. She had a long scar running along the inner half of her left arm. It looked as if the entire ulna had been removed.

31
The Crests of the Provinces of Canada

We decided against taking the ferry across to Ohio. The schedules were just too awkward. The kids were disappointed but we told them there was a ferry marked on the map at Amherstburg at the very end of Lake Erie. We'd zip across there.

So we drove along beautiful sunny Highways 18 and 18A past black families from Detroit fishing in roadside pools where egrets and herons brooded, past fruit farms and small fields of tomatoes, fields swarming with poor-looking families of pickers, past huge cottages owned by Americans and flying the US flag, past monasteries and convents with the everblue Lake Erie to the left sitting there like a handful of holy water held up to the parched lips of God.

We stopped at a little place called Colchester situated on a sort of nipple on the long breast-like curve of shore bulging out into the lake from Point Pelee to Windsor. We walked down to the water and waded a bit. There was a small house trailer set there on the lake, almost on the beach itself. The wheels had been removed and it looked as if it were there to stay.

A wooden patio had been built on one side of the trailer. The wood was painted in red and white stripes. There was an ornate railing running around the patio on three sides. Attached to the railing were several handpainted crests, one for each of the Canadian provinces. There was a large Canadian flag attached to the top of the trailer. And there was a small picket fence, about a foot high, marking what appeared to be the boundaries of the owner's property.

I was looking at the crests, from a respectful distance, when the owner pulled up on a bicycle. He was in his mid-thirties.

'Did you paint those crests?' I said.

'Yes, I sure did! You could tell he thought he'd done a marvellous job, and he had.

'They're really nice.'

'Thank you.' He looked thoughtful. 'Thank you.'

'What kind of paint did you use?'

'Any scraps I could get my hands on.'

'You mean house paint?'

'Yep. Mostly from neighbours. Scraping the bottoms of cans that people were finished with. Stuff like that.'

'Well they're really nice', I said. 'It's nice to see a patriotic man ... in this country.'

With that he really brightened up. 'I had two others but they blew away in a storm. We get some awful storms around here.'

'Which two?'

'The Northwest Territories and the Yukon.'

'Hmm! Isn't that strange? The only two that don't represent real provinces blow away.'

'We get some awful storms', he repeated. He sat on his bike and looked at me. He had chocolate brown eyes. 'This American and his wife were coming through one day', he said, 'and stopped. He knew Canada pretty well but his wife knew nothing about it. She was from Oklahoma or somewhere and thought the world ended at the American border. Well, he had me get all the crests and lay them down on the ground and go over each one with her, telling her the name of the province and the symbolism of the crest. I tell you, by the time I was finished she knew a lot about Canada.'

'I bet she did', I said. 'By the way, which crest gave you the most trouble?' There was a lovely breeze coming off the lake.

'To paint, you mean?'

'Yeah.'

'I'd say Manitoba there. I had a helluva time with that damned buffalo. You have no idea.'

32
Bruce
Eats
Stones

We had parked on a gravel road and tied Bruce to the side of the car. We left him with a bowl of dog food and a bowl of water. When we got back we noticed he was doing something funny. He was eating stones.

He had taken the stones from the road and put them in his bowl, just pushed the stones up into the bowl with his snout. Then he ate the food together with the stones.

We grabbed the bowl off him and picked out all the stones. Then we put the bowl down again.

And again he started nosing stones up into the bowl. And eating them with his food.

33

Ferry to Nowhere

When we got to Amherstburg there were no signs showing where the ferry dock was located so we drove down to the waterfront where a 300-pound black woman dressed in a pink pantsuit and a pink sunhat was sitting on the dock fishing with a bamboo pole ten feet long. She had just caught a fingerling and was gingerly trying to remove it from the hook. It looked as if the fish had swallowed the entire hook and the hook had pierced its little heart.

A white woman of about fifty years was standing there with her son – or was it her lover? He was about twenty. She kept touching his bare shoulders lovingly, lightly, teasingly. I couldn't tell whether she was trying to tease herself or him. She couldn't understand what I was asking her.

'The ferry dock? What do you mean, dear?' Her lipstick was smudged.

'The dock where the ferry boat pulls in to pick up passengers,' I said. I knew there was one because it was clearly marked on my road map. Well, fairly clearly.

'The dock for the ferry boat? What do you mean, dear?'

'Oh, forget it.' I started walking away and she called me back. Her young lover looked so serious.

'Oh, I know what you're looking for,' she said. 'It's half-a-mile back that way, dear,' she said. 'Yes, it's a half-a-mile back, dear.'

'Half-a-mile back?'

'Yes, dear.'

'That way?'

'Yes, dear.'

So we went back and sure enough we had gone right by it without noticing it. But that was because it wasn't really the sort of thing we were looking for. For one thing, it wasn't a car ferry. It was just a passenger ferry. And it didn't go right across the river to the United States. It just went over to an island in the river on the Canadian side where there was an amusement park, a private commercial establishment.

We had passed the signs advertising the amusement park and luckily the kids hadn't noticed them. It seemed odd that this would be marked on an official road map as a real ferry.

The signs advertised a duck that played the piano, a pig that tap-danced, and other 'feed-and-touch animals'. God, now we were trapped. The kids wanted to go.

'Does this ferry go across to the United States?' I asked the woman at the gate, who reminded me of the woman at the Point Pelee gatehouse. But this one had an English accent.

'No. It just goes to the island and the island is still in Canada,' she said. I could tell by the tone of her voice that she wanted me to know she was a nationalist and thought I was a traitor to want to go to the United States when Canada was so beautiful and even had an amusement park with real live feed-and-touch animals. 'It's still only in Canada,' she said, a little sarcastically.

'Oh Dad, let's go,' said Alison.

'Yeah Dad, come on,' said Jennifer.

'No, kids,' said Joan, saving my bacon again. 'We're going all the way around Lake Erie and we don't want to waste time in an amusement park. There will be lots of nicer places than this to visit when we get over to the States.'

Hmm!

In every city in Canada the poor people live in the north and east ends – except for Windsor. Here the really rundown areas are in the south and west ends. But the east and north ends don't look particularly prosperous either.

34
Windsor: The Gateway to the North

Windsor is the saddest city. Nowhere is Canada's plight more obvious. No matter where you are in town you can look up and see the huge Ambassador Bridge to Detroit rainbowing through the air like a cultural and economic syphon. The bridge doesn't seem to link two pieces of land. Rather it seems to link two levels of land. It's the highest thing in Windsor and the lowest thing in Detroit.

Indeed, the United States from this vantage point gives the distinct impression of being some magic land in the clouds, the magic bridge streaming down from these clouds and condescending to land in the hinterlands, this inferior, non-descript underworld where the land has long been permanently scorched.

And from everywhere in Windsor you can see the skyline of Detroit. Everytime you look up there it is. In Vancouver when you look up you see the mountains. In Windsor when you look up you see Detroit.

As if that weren't enough Detroit is upwind of Windsor. Every fart, every belching smokestack comes drifting like a putrid inescapable river into Windsor. And if you turn on the radio you'll be lucky if you find a little Canadian station in between the giant American ones, sandwiched like an earwig between pairs of copulating elephants.

It's a nice place to visit though. And there are several good American and British writers living in Windsor.

35

What to Wear When You Visit the United States

And for our last supper in Canada we went to the Top Hat Restaurant on University Avenue. It was quite a posh restaurant. There were suits of armour standing around in the foyer looking sadly important. In the washroom there was a blackboard with chalk and eraser and a sign saying FOR POETS & ARTISTS. There were lots of different rooms, lounges and so on. The cutlery, china and furniture was old, rich and well-maintained. The walls were made from pieces of coloured glass and old wine bottles with light shining through. It doesn't take much to make me happy. And the matchbooks. The matchbooks were in the shape of a top hat and bore the slogan: LOBSTERS ENTERTAINMENT NIGHTLY.

'What do you think lobsters entertainment is like?' I asked the kids.

'Maybe they tap-dance on their pinchers,' said Jennifer.

'They probably square-dance underwater,' said Alison.

'I bet they do Al Jolson imitations to keep from being boiled alive,' said Joan.

The kids were fooling around with the cigarette machine and found a quarter in the return slot. They gave it to the bartender. He was appreciative. 'You have very nice kids,' he said. He had a Clark Gable moustache. He looked like a refugee from Detroit.

On the way out I looked at the suits of armour and shuddered. Maybe we should get four of these for our trip through the States, I thought. I didn't say anything though.

36

A Horrible Way to Die

I felt a little uneasy. Was I doing the right thing in taking my kids to the United States again?

Of course I was. I simply had to learn to disregard my paranoid feelings about this monstrous country. As Canadians we tend to look at the American underbelly with more loathing than it deserves. For the real people of the earth there are no borders. For the poor people of the world the world is an open book.

But I was thinking of that poor kid from Hamilton who went to Florida on his motorcycle and was found shot to death on the side of the road in Ohio. He had probably made a rude gesture to a motorist who had cut him off and the motorist retaliated by blowing his head off with a shotgun. But a killing like this could have taken place anywhere – even in Canada. The European races, famed and feared for hundreds of years for their ferocious war-like nature, have shown signs recently of regaining their sanity, of becoming, once again, like all the other races.

But I'm far off the track. As we left the Top Hat Restaurant I asked the others if they wanted to enter the United States via the Ambassador Bridge or the Detroit Tunnel. And after lengthy discussion as befits such a momentous decision they opted for the tunnel. But there were certain misgivings.

The entrance to the tunnel was just a few blocks from the restaurant. We followed the signs, then paid our seventy-five cents. As we approached the dark entrance I suddenly remembered something horrible from my childhood. It must have been connected with the birth trauma. My mother told me I had an easy birth, but what does she know?

At any rate I could remember as a child fantasizing about the various ways of dying. And I decided the worst possible way, worse even than a plane crash or falling from a trapeze, would be to have a tunnel cave in on you as you were driving through. Particularly a tunnel under a river. I'd never been to Detroit but I'd heard of this horrible tunnel.

But that was ridiculous. Do you realize what the odds would be against this tunnel collapsing during the few minutes it would take you to drive through? Don't even think of such a preposterous idea.

But somehow Joan picked up my thoughts. On the road were some puddles of water illuminated by ghostly yellow light and Joan said, 'Where is that water coming from?'

A chill ran up my back. We were obviously having the same fantasy. She thought the entire Detroit River was about to come cascading in and sweep us away like so much flotsam and jetsam. Another memory from my childhood: When I was a kid I had a book called *Flotsam and Jetsam*. It was a totally ordinary book but I loved it. It was about a guy who loved his sailboat. He used to sail out in the harbour first thing in the morning and write down his thoughts. One line I particularly remember went like this: 'It was a beautiful sunrise this morning ... for those of us awake to enjoy it.' I never did find out the name of the writer because the book was missing its cover before it came into my hands. But he was *really* human. If anyone reading this knows anything about that particular book I'd appreciate a note. Just write me care of my publisher, whoever it might be.

'It's just rainwater,' I said. We were sailing through the tunnel like a motorized mole.

43

'How could rainwater get in here?' said Joan. She seemed on the verge of clutching my arm and screaming: 'Get me out of here right now!'

'I don't know. It just does. Rain falls on the street and seeps down here because it's lower.'

'But it's not raining, there's no rain on the street.'

'That's because it's all evaporated but this is a tunnel and the water doesn't evaporate as quickly.'

37

A Reasonable Request for Oranges

I don't think my explanation really satisfied Joan, and I know it didn't totally satisfy myself, but there was light at the end of the tunnel. And soon a customs official bathed in sunlight was leaning in the window and asking me for my birth certificate.

'By golly, I left it at home,' I said. 'It's in my fireproof filing cabinet.'

'That's not much good to you there,' she said. She was beautiful, or would be if it weren't for the mean look on her face. She figured she was smarter than me.

'The last time we came over you didn't require a birth certificate so I didn't bother bringing it this time.'

'Birth certificates have been required to cross into the United States at Detroit for almost two years.'

'Well, I'll be.'

She spoke rather sarcastically and it appeared as if we were going to be turned back at the border, refused entry to the USA. But then she asked for our dog's needle certificates and we had all that in order. She found nothing amiss there. How could she have known that the vet's signature had been forged? Then she asked if we had any oranges.

'That's *all* you asked the last time we came over. Do you have any oranges? We said no and you waved us on.'

'I wasn't working here that long ago.'

'Oh, I'm sorry. I didn't mean you *personally*. I meant you *plural*. I guess I should have said *youse*.'

'There's a lot of cars behind you. Do you have any oranges?'

'No.'

'Okay, move ahead.'

'Oh by the way, do you know where we can get a map of Michigan?'

'Try a service station. Now move it!'

I went to pull away and stalled the van. Then we jerked away through the rain puddles out onto the streets of Detroit. 'What a bitch!' said Joan. 'We should report her. Did you get her badge number? She didn't have to be that nasty.'

'I wonder why they always ask about oranges?' I said.

There were no service stations within sight and so, remembering vaguely the route from our trip to Florida of a few years earlier (you can read an account of that trip in a poem called 'A Typical Canadian Family Visits Disney World', in *A Knight in Dried Plums*), we headed out onto the Interstate 75 heading south towards the Ohio border. We wanted to stay off the expressways but this was the only road heading around the western end of Lake Erie.

No sooner did we get onto the expressway than we became entangled in heavy fast-moving traffic, were forced to make a premature exit, and found ourselves in the heart of downtown Detroit.

It was just like a 1936 Hollywood movie. But there were no young James Cagneys or Clark Gables running around. There were just a lot of boarded-up windows and padlocked doors. And a lot of black people standing around waiting for buses.

Another funny story from my childhood came to mind: I was sitting in the Detroit bus terminal. It was the summer of 1959. The place was crowded but there was an empty seat next to me. On the other side of the empty seat a nice-looking middle-aged businessman was reading newspapers and piling them up on the vacant seat. A big fat black girl came up to him and pointed at his papers. 'Do you mind if I sit there, sir?' she said.

With that the guy stood up, picked up all the newspapers and in a fit of temper threw them across the floor of the bus terminal. Then he stalked off, black smoke puffing out his ears. The black girl looked hurt and sad, but she was relieved to be able to sit down at last. I would have said something to her like, 'Don't let that nasty bastard bother you', but a lot of people had been warning me not to talk to black people in too friendly a way. It might cause a fight. This was a long time ago of course. I'd been on the bus from Chicago to Detroit and was sitting next to a beautiful black girl about my age: late teens. My heart was thumping and I kept trying to engage her in conversation but she wouldn't speak. Then she fell asleep. And as she did her lovely little head came to rest on my shoulder. I was thrilled as only an innocent, pure-hearted eighteen-year-old could be.

I happened to look up towards the front of the bus and saw **45** something funny happen. The bus driver noticed us through the rearview mirror, noticed her head on my shoulder, and did a classic double take. The bus almost went off the road. Others noticed as well and soon I was getting all kinds of dirty looks. I mean I didn't *have* to be sitting next to this *black* girl. There were all kinds of other empty seats. When she woke up and found her head had been on my shoulder she moved closer to the window and cried. I'd tried to comfort her but she was impossible.

When the bus stopped at South Bend, Indiana, or Kalamazoo, Michigan, or some place like that a bunch of hostile looking guys crowded around me and wanted to know where I came from. When I told them they seemed to sympathize with me a bit. They warned me I'd likely get killed if I kept on acting that way.

I was shattered. When I got back on the bus I sat by myself. The black girl wouldn't talk to me anyway. Perhaps I wouldn't have been such a moral coward if she'd expressed some interest.

But that was such a long time ago. It makes me feel not only like an old man but also as if I've been wasting my life. Ah, but who cares? To waste your life is a totally European concept anyway, coldly neurotic. Thinking about the past is also a sign of brain malfunction, European-style.

And back in the beautiful moment ... but wait! Even as I write this I realize I'm thinking about the past, writing about the past. Things are happening around me as I type but I have excluded them from consciousness: the sunlight filtering through the small bottle collection on the windowsill, the beautiful blue of the walls, the sound the typewriter makes, the sound the spring birds out there make, the telephone that rings occasionally, the conversations I have. None of this is going into my writing. I'm writing about something that happened months ago. The kids have come home for lunch and are making lunch for themselves and asking if I want a sandwich. But I am caught in the past, trying to fix a moment that has already become totally dead. The one saving grace is that I have a book full of notes taken as the incidents unfolded. And now I'm engaged in a typing and editing pattern more than a writing pattern. And the typing and the editing are taking place in the present.

And the end result of course will be to take something from the past, in this case a trip around Lake Erie in the summer of 1977, and make it permanently a feature of the endlessly unrolling present by writing about it and having it in a book that will never recede into the past. So that 1977, for me, will never be totally dead. And so somehow that justifies what doesn't really need to be justified anyway. 'Only a man harrowing clods in a slow silent walk? My life would be somewhat poorer if Thomas Hardy hadn't written that poem. And he didn't write it in the present so to speak. He saw it, then thought about it for a while before setting it on paper. And he was a European.

So before we managed to get back on to the southbound expressway we made quite a thorough tour of downtown Detroit. I'd heard some awful things about it but it seemed pretty ordinary to me. I got the impression all the really run-down slums were inhabited by people of European descent. The more expensive-looking areas with stately, well-maintained, brown-brick buildings from the turn of the century and with well-maintained lawns and gardens were inhabited by people of African descent. The whites we saw looked like winos, the blacks like successful businessmen. There seemed to be a lot of poverty in all the sections we passed through but it was the whites who were the victims rather than the blacks. Ridiculous making comments like this based on such scanty evidence. But there comes a time in a writer's life when he has to give up any lingering reluctance to appear ridiculous.

We passed Tiger Stadium, home of the Detroit Tigers, and the Olympiad, home of the Detroit Red Wings, and finally found our way back onto the Interstate 75. The Ambassador Bridge brooded in the background. At one point in our misdirection we found ourselves heading on the expressway to Chicago and we considered going there just for the hell of it but decided it wouldn't look good in a story about a trip around Lake Erie. I figure a writer should have some kind of respect for his readers if he wants to have any and I do, I do.

39

The Monroe K-Mart and Garage

We were travelling south-southwest along the flat ledge-back of Lake Erie and we were getting occasional glimpses of that tranquil freshwater inland sea. The last time we drove this way it was February and a huge snowstorm came up. Giant tractor-trailers were jackknifing all over the place and our little Toyota gave up the ghost on the 75 near Lima, Ohio. But this was summer and Lake Erie was winking at us conspiratorially, as if to say you are the only ones who really know me. To these Americans I'm just a body (of water) but you Canadians know my true soul. There's something unreal about the United States.

We stopped at a K-Mart in Monroe, Michigan. Joan wanted to get some camping supplies. The place was crowded with Americans. I kept wondering if people could tell we were foreigners. I was really self-conscious. I wanted to have a pee and found out I had to apply at a special window for permission to enter the public washroom. The girl in the window looked at me blankly, figured I was no security risk, and pressed a buzzer which unlocked the washroom door. The cubicles were painted dark brown. The graffiti was decidedly strange. 'I'm going to see the Teasers tonight and don't try to stop me' someone had written.

When I came out there was a short crippled girl staring at me. She was really beautiful and wore crutches with special arm braces. Both legs seemed to be useless. Her eyes shone and she licked her lips as she looked at me. She must have been about seventeen. I walked over to the stereo department. They had some really expensive equipment in stock. As I watched a young fellow about nineteen came in, looked at a set and bought it. He wrote a cheque for $650 and walked out with the set in a huge carton. Monroe is basically a Detroit suburb and I guess a lot of the people work in the motor plants. And who knows, that guy might have been looking at that particular set for a week.

The rear-view mirror on the passenger's side of our van had become loose and on the way out I stopped at the K-Mart garage and asked to borrow a wrench. The mechanic was quite generous about it.

'You certainly may, sir', he said.

He handed me the wrench with no questions asked and I walked out with it and tightened the mirror.

'Thanks', I said when I gave him back the wrench.

'Don't mention it.'

Americans are friendly people.

40
The Androids
of Luna Pier

We didn't bother stopping at the General Custer Historic Site, nor at the 'Frozen Custer' stand nearby. We drove straight back to the Interstate 75 but after a few miles of fast driving I noticed we were low on gas so we had to get off again.

We took the next exit and found ourselves in a place called Luna Pier, a small resort community right on the lake. It was a strange-looking place with a series of scum-covered canals heading nowhere and people repairing the roofs of their cottages. Women in sausage pincurls were standing in the middle of the road talking. I don't know what they were talking about. Maybe they were talking about us.

'Yes, there's a family of Canadians coming through in a yellow

van. Here they come now. They're very superior, they think they own the entire rights to Lake Erie. They think we're unreal, somnambulistic, living out our dull lives like meaningless androids.'

'How do you know all this?'

'I picked it up on my sausage pincurls.'

The women smiled mechanically and moved to the side of the road to let us through.

The Luna Pier gas station was hopelessly crowded. It was the only one around for miles. Everyone was smoking around the pumps. I started to get nervous. We waited in line for about fifteen minutes.

There was a midget pumping gas. He had a high forehead and was puffing furiously on a midget cigar. I handed him my Chargex card and asked if he honoured it. He couldn't make up his mind and kept turning it over and over. He was puffing so hard on his little cigar flames and sparks were coming out the end. I thought the place was going to blow up. Things like that are always happening in the United States. Two paragraphs in the *Toronto Star*. So I finally said, 'If you have to think about it, it's no good', grabbed the Chargex card out of his pudgy little hand, and drove off.

We drove inland about ten miles to the town of Samaria before we found another gas station. We filled up and got a map.

'I'm glad I don't have to live in that crummy place', said Joan, referring to Luna Pier.

I remembered an English friend of mine coming to Canada. He asked me if I would be able to tell he was English just by seeing him on the street. You would be able to tell, but I didn't tell him. He had a certain different way of holding his facial muscles, a slightly different way of walking.

'That's the way I felt in that ᴋ-Mart', I told Joan. 'I kept wondering if people knew I was Canadian.' She said she didn't feel that way at all. In fact most of the time she wasn't conscious of being outside her own country.

As for Luna Pier, I told her she would probably have loved the place if it had been in Canada. It was just the knowledge that it was in the United States that made her dislike it so much.

'Oh no', she said. 'You're dead wrong there.'

I turned on the radio. 'One out of every six adults has high blood pressure', said the announcer.

41
High Blood Pressure

42

Charging Admission to See an Earthquake Crack

We cut down to Toledo on the 75 then drove right through the city and across the Maumee River. If you think of Lake Erie as a mouse, then the Maumee River is the mouse's tail. That's the way it looks on the map anyway. The river starts up somewhere in Indiana.

Soon we were out of Toledo and heading east along the US 280 through the town of Oregon then down to the US 2. The US 2 parallels the south shore of Lake Erie but for the most part not close enough to see the water. Marshy land surrounded the highway and as you drove along you could pick out dozens of varieties of ducks, herons and other water birds. The kids dozed off in the back seat and Joan put her head down on my lap and fell asleep.

At one point we passed a nuclear power plant featuring a huge eggcup-shaped building about 500 feet high. A really massive thing. It looked as if it had been built by the same guy who builds the McDonald's hamburg places. It had been up quite a while and there had been no maintenance at all. The signs had fallen off. Even the paint was falling off in huge flakes like falling leaves. But the paint was green, which is the colour of leaves but not of falling leaves. I wanted to stop and take a picture of it but I didn't want to awaken Joan and the kids. It looked like the sort of place where you could drive in and get fast service on a small nuclear bomb. It looked as if you could pick up a case of leukemia just by leaning against the fence.

We passed Crane Creek State Beach and the towns of Long Beach and Locust Point. At this point there's an interesting peninsula that juts out into Lake Erie, surrounded by four islands. I'd noticed it on the map many times in the past but never visualized myself being there. I mean, why would I? It's due south of Point Pelee and Pelee Island and forms part of the partial land bridge across western Lake Erie, the flyway which migrating birds find so attractive.

As we drove through Port Clinton and further out along the Marblehead Peninsula it became apparent we were heading into tourist country. It was highly commercialized in a way that Point Pelee definitely was not, though Point Pelee definitely attracts tourists.

Most of the tourism around Marblehead though was of the short-run, day-trip variety. Mostly holidaying Ohio residents. I can't imagine people from other states saying hey, let's head up to Lake Erie for our holidays this year.

Cottages, trailer camps, and tourist traps of all kinds became more and more frequent. Highway signs advertised the attractions. Everything was amazing and unbelievable and fantastic.

The AMAZING PREHISTORIC VALLEY was straight ahead. You could turn left for the FANTASTIC EARTHQUAKE CRACK – BRING YOUR CAMERA.

The largest granite cut in Canada is on Ontario Highway 118 just west of Bracebridge but there are no signs pointing it out. The skull-like Bruce's Cave, on the Bruce Peninsula, stares out across the Canadian Shield towards Labrador as if waiting longingly for the return of the Ice Age. It's marked by a feeble little cardboard hand-written sign nailed to a stunted sumach. I remember climbing a medium-size mountain near Banff and finding, when I got to the top, there was a chair-lift I could have taken. I hadn't noticed it. But at the summit were dozens of US tourists milling around. You could see for a hundred miles in any direction. It was glorious. One of the Americans sneered, kicked a small rock and said, 'I suppose they'll eventually get this place cleaned up.'

43

Americans Are Even Friendlier When Drunk

On our Boron map of the eastern states there was a red dot marked East Harbor State Park. It was halfway between Port Clinton and the town of Marblehead. The map didn't really seem all that accurate though.

We drove past an unmarked state park. It was about seven o'clock. So we turned into a side road in order to turn around and go back. Another car pulled in alongside ours. Two guys were in it.

'What are you lookin' for?' the guy on the passenger side said. He had blue eyes, sort of unfocussed, and he talked as if he were slightly drunk. But he obviously wanted to help.

'We were just turning around to go back to the state park.'

'Go straight ahead,' he said. He conferred for a moment with the driver, a darker fellow with a whacky grin. 'Go down to the stop-light then turn left. It'll take you to East Harbor State Park. That's where you want to go.'

'Thanks a lot. That's where we were heading but we passed another state park a mile or so back. It wasn't marked on the map. We were just turning back to check it out.'

'You can't camp there,' he said. 'But you can camp all night at East Harbor State Park.'

'Thanks a lot, eh?' I said. Americans love to hear Canadians say 'eh?' They smiled. They had huge beer bellies, like Georgia sherrifs. Then they drove down the sideroad, weaving a bit from side to side.

I pulled back onto the highway and headed east towards the stoplight.

'Were they drunk?' said Joan.

'Just a little bit maybe,' I said.

The kids giggled.

Canadians Are Really Cute

But we were out of luck. East Harbor State Park was filled to capacity for the night. We'd heard on our car radio all along that hotels, motels, tourist homes and campgrounds were all filled up and people had been sleeping in their cars at the side of the road. It was the July 4 weekend. People were on the move. It was the 201st birthday of the United States of America. *Ta-ta!* Tell that to the Indians.

Joan was getting a little edgy. She said we should have started looking for a campsite at five o'clock. 'I don't want to leave it this late any more.' We kept passing motels and campgrounds with NO VACANCY signs. Every time we saw another NO VACANCY sign Joan would sigh.

We stopped at Camp Runnamuck. The guy said he had nothing but he could let us park at the side of the road with no shade and no picnic table. Joan wouldn't go for it. There was a sign saying NO ROWDYISM. 'Why don't you just kick out some of the rowdies and let us have their spot?' I said.

'You Canadians are really cute,' he said. I wondered if he could tell I was a Canadian because of my accent. Or maybe he'd noticed my licence plate: KEEP ONTARIO BEAUTIFUL.

45
October 8, 1686

It was a beautiful area, really. It was the hour before sundown and the little towns radiated a pristine beauty. People walked along the streets in a trance. Everyone looked as if he or she had just stepped out of a shower and put on fresh clothing.

We finally found a place called Ned's Ledge just past Marblehead at the tip of this lovely peninsula separating Lake Erie from Sandusky Bay. We were almost due south of Pelee Island. In fact looking out over the lake I thought I saw Pelee Island in the late afternoon sun. It looked the same as it had from the other side, from the west beach of Point Pelee, earlier that day in the early morning sun with Bruce rolling over and over on the dead fish. We could also see Johnson's Island which contains the ruins of a Civil War prison and cemetery.

The woman's name was Shirley. She charged us $3.00 and wrote us a receipt. What looked like a seventeenth-century grave marker was propped against a tree outside the house. But it was only a copy. Shirley's husband had cut it from a slab of wood. 'Ned's good at that sort of thing. He really is. But he doesn't do it much anymore,' she said. 'He's too busy all the time.' She sounded as if she wished he'd slow down.

Here is what the grave marker said:

JANE SECORD

WIFE TO CAPT.

RICHARD MORE

SENr, AGED, 55

YEARS. DEPARTED

THIS LIFE YE

8 of OCTOBER

— 1686 —

We set up camp in the middle of a grassy field spread out behind Ned and Shirley's white frame house. I always feel a little stupid at moments like this. It somehow seems a little less natural than just turning in at a hotel or even a motel. A little less natural even though presumably you're closer to nature.

46

The World's Largest Movie Screen

Anyway it was the July 4 weekend and the other campers were flying US flags and tossing firecrackers. The kids ran across the field to play on the swings. I tied Bruce's leash to a stake. Joan made some sandwiches. I got the sleeping gear ready.

Then came one of the bonuses of this kind of trip: the friendliness of the people. You get to make friends wherever you go. A woman, one of the campers, came over to talk to us. Things like this never happen in motels or hotels.

The woman's name was Evelyn. She brought over her shy little girl, Kelly, and her not-so-shy brown dog, Rusty. She told us they'd had a tornado just last week.

'Too bad my friend Russell wasn't here,' I said. 'He's crazy about tornadoes but he's never seen one.'

'He wouldn't have been able to see it if he was here,' she said without smiling. 'It was in the middle of the night.'

She and her husband were planning to take their kids to Cedar Point the next day. Cedar Point was apparently a semi-Disneyland. They wanted to leave first thing in the morning because it was expensive. Admission was $8.50 per person. They wanted to spend a full day there to make sure they got their money's worth. The parents were more excited than the kids.

She was really surprised we hadn't heard about Cedar Point.

You could tell she was thinking unpleasant thoughts about the intelligence of Canadians. 'They just have the world's largest movie screen there, that's all,' she said. 'Six stories high!'

She went on to tell us about all the amusements and rides they have there. She told us that every morning in the summer there's a line-up of cars five miles long waiting to get in. We had no reason to disbelieve her. She said she'd been to Point Pelee when she was a kid.

'Want to go?' I asked Joan after the woman left. Meaning to Cedar Point the next day.

'No thanks,' said Joan.

I was glad. I always get sick on rides. Even ferris wheels. Or, as the kids used to call them, fairest wheels.

47

Why Bruce Likes to Roll Over on Dead Fish and Eat Stones

An older man and woman came by. They were in their sixties. They had a brown dog with them, part Labrador retriever and part collie. Its name was Rusty.

'That woman who was just over here had a dog named Rusty,' I said.

'Popular name for dogs,' he said.

'A pop pup name,' said Alison.

They were nice, intelligent people and the woman reminded me a lot of Joan's mother. But they frightened me a little because they thought Canada should be taken over by the United States as soon as possible because of all the communists up there. I just smiled and agreed pleasantly because Joan was giving me significant glances and meaningful looks.

The old fellow said the socialist policies of Trudeau's government were going to destroy Canada economically. He seemed to be genuinely concerned about the fate of Canada. He said he and his wife had long been thinking of taking a motor trip into Canada but hadn't got around to it yet. Maybe next summer.

It turned out this man, whose name was Clive, knew a lot about dogs. Of course, you might say, Americans know a lot about everything. But he seemed to know his dogs all right.

He told us Bruce likes to roll over on dead fish because he wants to get their smell on his fur. It's a way of disguising his own smell so that other animals will be confused. The average dog's mind is quite devious when it comes to other dogs. And of course the average dog's mind is located in his nose.

As for pushing stones up into his food bowl, that's just the dog's instinct which tells it to bury its food. He probably is not really eating the stones, he just appears to be. He is probably nosing the stones out of the way and eating the food – that is, unburying the food and eating it. Maybe a few go down but it won't hurt him any, Clive said.

We were still a little worried but he said we shouldn't be. 'A dog's instinct will keep it out of trouble a lot better than a human's instinct will, he said, ambiguously.

He seemed to be tremendously well-informed on politics and animals.

'You should have your own talk show, I said.

Meanwhile, Bruce was tugging at his stake trying to get a shot at Rusty. Rusty was about three times Bruce's size. But Bruce was baring his fangs and growling at him.

So much for Bruce's instincts. He plays with cats, ignores small dogs, and fearlessly attacks large dogs.

48
Gratuitous Violence

After the kids were in bed Joan and I sat under the full moon. Among other things that must remain unrecorded, unless as some people say everything we say, do or think is recorded forever by a giant recorder in heaven or in another dimension closer to us than our skin, we talked about the United States.

Joan spoke of how awful it must be to be an American, hated by the rest of the world.

'In their own country they go out of their way to be generous, sweet and gentle, she purred. She said they seem to be unusually self-conscious about their nationality.

I didn't know about that. Whenever you say anything about a race the opposite becomes equally true. All I know is that there is an overpowering sense of boredom in the American air. You feel it, at least I do, as soon as you cross the border. I remember feeling it on my first trip to the United States when I was twelve. For a Canadian the United States is an exotic country and any Canadian travelling through the United States is bound to have a sense of déjà-vu about many of the things he sees, as if they were seen before in old Hollywood movies. But that doesn't negate the boredom that hangs so heavy in the air. It's as if all the beauty and excitement one would expect has been harvested by the American film industry, leaving nothing but despair.

Canada is a much more exciting country in every way. At least that's the way I felt in the summer of 1977. There is something unformed about Canada. But the only people who are doing anything are real estate developers and entrepreneurs of various kinds who don't give a damn about anything except profits.

For an American, despair sets in early, perhaps even before

puberty. There's simply nothing left to do. How boring it must be. It's just the same old thing over and over.

Americans always seem to be hurrying home to watch television.

The only thing left is gratuitous violence.

The Ghost of Jane Secord

It was the evening of July 2, 1977. Near Marblehead, Ohio, Ned's Ledge was situated on a height of land from which could be seen large stretches of Lake Erie and Sandusky Bay. It was a fairly prosperous area. American flags were flying everywhere.

The first loud bang came around eight o'clock. By sundown huge skyrockets were soaring through the air and exploding in red, white and blue orgasms. In the campgrounds at Ned's Ledge one camper called several of his neighbours over to help him set up a large heavy American flag. He wanted it placed on top of his motor home. The flag was so heavy it looked as if it were going to make the motor home tip over.

No one would be able to accuse this man of being unamerican. He was proud of his country and cherished the freedoms guaranteed to him by the American constitution. But the enemies of the American way of life were many. Their motivation was not easy to understand but it probably had something to do with envy.

Later I dreamt that the McFaddens were sleeping in their camping van, which wasn't all that strange because we were. And suddenly the door opened. It sounded so realistic I woke up and checked the doors. They were closed. No one was stirring around the van. So I went back to sleep.

About an hour later Joan woke up and said she just heard the door open. I heard it too. It really sounded realistic. But when I checked the doors they were tightly closed and there didn't seem to be anyone stirring around the van. The same story. It didn't occur to me to lock the doors.

We talked about it in the morning. Why should we both have the auditory hallucination that the doors were being opened? Joan said she lay awake for hours expecting someone to open the door and blast us with a shotgun. Only in America could such fears exist in peacetime.

'Why didn't you ask me to lock the doors?'

'I didn't think of it.'

A provincial cabinet minister from the Hamilton area once publically accused the US television networks of conspiring to feature so many shows depicting violence in American life, exaggerating the frequency and intensity of such violence to such a degree that viewers would be conditioned into thinking it was unsafe to go on the streets at night. This was intended to encourage people to stay home and watch television so that the ratings would go up.

But when you look at the statement it can be boiled down to the same old story: the United States isn't such a bad place really. We should establish ever closer ties. It would be good for business.

Anyway the guy lost his seat in the next election. Probably more because he was always advocating curfews for teenagers. I mean, who wants teenagers hanging around the house? He was also trying to pass a bill requiring teenagers to carry ID cards.

I kept thinking about that door opening. Could it have been the ghost of Jane Secord, wandering hopelessly over the face of the earth for 291 years, searching for the guy who made a duplicate of her grave marker?

50
When a Poet
Gets a Grant

Off and on for the past year I've been working on the details of a plan that would result, if successful, in great masses of people suddenly paying more attention to the poets of Anglo Canada. The manipulation of the mass mind. Unfortunately I'm not at liberty to divulge details of my plan at this time.

But on the train of civilization, newspapers, television, and other forms of pop culture are in the caboose. The poets are up front in the engine compartment. They may not be giving us much direction but at least they are the first to glimpse where we're going.

Ah, to be able to live off royalties! Grants are wonderful, but for every dollar that goes to a poet there's a hundred thousand dollars going to the vast artistic institutions built upon his vision.

The Hamilton *Spectator,* which advocates economic union with the US, recently ran an editorial saying it was okay for the Canada Council to give money to theatre groups, art galleries and symphony orchestras but grants to individual artists were simply 'protecting mediocrity,' and simply an excuse for the artist 'to do his own thing.'

So I fired off a letter to the editor asking where theatre groups and symphony orchestras would perform and what art galleries would show without the work of individual artists. And I told them they were saying that just because theatre groups, art galleries and symphony orchestras advertise in the newspapers while individual artists don't.

I was particularly mad because they ran the editorial shortly after running a news story about me getting a grant. The news story was written in such a way that it would be bound to annoy a lot of people, as if it were begging people to be annoyed. I felt as if I'd been exploited to help sell papers.

When a poet gets a grant he is somehow reduced to the status of an institution and a minor one at that.

51
The Power and the Glory

Shirley and Ned were up early in the morning. They were getting ready for a garage sale. They had a back massager that was only used once, and some books by Billy Graham and Barry Goldwater. They also had firewood and ice for sale and cottages and boats for rent.

Ned taught English in the local high school, the largest high school in Ohio. He was the head of the English department. 'I supervise twenty-four English teachers', he said.

'That's strange', I said. Ned looked at me. 'I know a fellow who teaches English in a high school in Picton, Ontario, and he looks remarkably like you.' It was true. Ned looked a little like Dirk Bogarde as well, but sadder and with slightly less of an international look about him somehow, more of a heartland USA look, a little more tired looking. As if he were dying before really having lived. I didn't want to tell him that though of course. I thought I'd go on and on and give him the impression that Canadians are tremendous bores.

'Actually this fellow, and I'm sorry I forgot his name, he's not from the Picton area – do you know where Picton is? No? It's on the north shore of Lake Ontario, on a peninsula that juts out into Lake Ontario just as Marblehead Peninsula juts out into Lake Erie. But this fellow, and my God he really resembles you, and him being an English teacher and all that, it's really strange, he was born and raised on an island in the Bay of Fundy.'

By this time I could see Ned's eyeballs were ready to explode. When is this guy going to shut up? he was saying to himself. Can't he see I've got a lot of things to do? God, Canadians are boring.

But as soon as I said the word Fundy I stopped talking and turned away. I started digging through the books and bought a copy of Graham Greene's *The Power and the Glory*. It was a dime. 'That's a good book', he said weakly. 'It's all about a priest.'

'Is it taught in your high school?'

'Yes, it's on one course.'

Yeah, I thought, an ideal book for high school. Pleases the Catholics because it's about a priest and pleases the non-Catholics because he's not a very good priest. And the teacher can go on and on about Greene's humanity until school's out and the kids head home to watch 'Starsky and Hutch' and 'Kojack' and 'Policewoman' on television. Another good novelist bites the dust. Like going before a firing squad.

Anyway it seemed as if Ned had solved some of life's problems. The purpose of life was to make money, at least in modest amounts. And since Ned was a quiet, peaceful man he had chosen quiet, peaceful ways to do so. I would love to know what the twenty-four English teachers think about him and his ledge and his garage sales and his campgrounds and his cottages and boats for rent and his firewood and ice and old Graham Greene novels for sale. Probably nothing at all.

I asked him about the grave marker. He said he did it ten years ago on a holiday trip through New England. It took him all day. He really enjoyed doing it but he didn't think he'd ever do anything like it again.

It occurs to me I may have let down my readers by not taking ferry rides to the various islands off Marblehead Peninsula. There certainly appears to be a lot to see on some of the larger islands of this group.

52 The Possibility of a Second Edition of This Book

For instance, Perry's Victory and the International Peace Memorial is located on South Bass Island which can be reached by ferry from either Port Clinton or Catawba. None of these islands is as large as Pelee Island on the Canadian side, but South Bass Island boasts a highway, US 357, and a town, Put-In Bay.

The largest of the group of islands is Kelleys Island which boasts a town of the same name and a highway, US 575. Glacial Grooves State Memorial Park is located on this island which can be reached by ferry from Sandusky or Marblehead. Inscription Rock State Memorial is also located on Kelleys Island.

The town of Middle Bass, Ohio, is located on Middle Bass Island which can be reached by ferry from South Bass Island. Isle Saint George is a town on North Bass Island but there is no ferry service. Other islands include Starve Island, Sugar Island, Middle Bass Island, Rattlesnake Island and Mouse Island.

I'm sure if I had visited these islands I would have gathered material that would have considerably enriched this book. And perhaps if sufficient response to this book is forthcoming, I might be encouraged to repeat my trip at greater leisure and with more thoroughness. Perhaps a second trip would yield much material that could be incorporated into a second edition.

Truthfully though I hadn't planned to explore the US side of Lake Erie. I merely wanted to motor around the lake to see, as I said before, what it looked like from the other side. US writers seem to be doing a more than adequate job of exploring their own country. If I wanted to do any detailed exploration of an area I think the area I would choose would be within the borders of my own country, Canada.

And if I may take this opportunity to speak of myself as a writer, I would say that in all my books there has been little exploration of the outer world – in the sense of physical exploration. My way has been to discuss in my writing the things that appear to me in the course of my ordinary existence – the things that find me rather than the things I find. I am a filter. I have to impose certain restrictions on myself if what I am to write is to be in any way intelligible. My choice of what restrictions to impose on myself defines me as a writer. My attitude has always been to treat writing as a peripheral enterprise. My writing has always been concerned with what I can see without turning my head.

After breakfast we broke camp and left Ned's Ledge forever. We drove along the north shore of Sandusky Bay. In the distance we could see the low level bridge which would soon take us across to the south shore and on to Sandusky. The area seemed a little remote and isolated. Yet it was good tourist attraction country. We passed colourful, imaginatively designed signs advertising things like SENECA CAVERNS RAIN OR SHINE, MYSTERY HILL SEE THE AMAZING FORCE OF GRAVITY, and PREHISTORIC FOREST BRING YOUR CAMERA.

53
World's Strangest Babies

Sandusky Bay is about three miles wide at this point and there are actually two causeways crossing it, running parallel and about a mile apart. We crossed on the older of the two, a two-laner. There was hardly any traffic on our causeway, which was part of US 269. But the traffic was bumper-to-bumper on the other causeway, part of US 2, a multi-lane controlled-access freeway stretching from Port Clinton to Huron and bypassing Sandusky.

After hitting dry land the road passes through the little towns of Bay View and Baybridge. Then I spotted a much more modest sign at the side of the road. Because of its small size and look of impermanence it immediately engaged my interest. It was merely an arrow pointing off down a dirt road. It bore the words WORLD'S STRANGEST BABIES.

I don't think Joan or the kids noticed the sign. I drove on, wondering. The words kept going over and over in my head: World's strangest babies, world's strangest babies. I spotted a miniature golf course ahead. 'Who'd like to play miniature golf?'

'Oh, could we, Mom?' said Alison. 'That would be nice.'

Joan looked at me strangely.

'Just you kids and Mommy. I have to go back on the road a bit. I'll be back in half an hour. Play good.'

Joan looked at me even more strangely.

'It's just something I want to see, something I'm curious about but it's nothing that would interest you or the kids. I'll tell you about it when I get back.'

'Dave?'

'Yes?' I knew she was going to say be careful.

'Be careful, okay?'

'Okay. I'll be back in less than half an hour. Don't worry. Enjoy your game.'

54
A Non-Profit Educational Story

The dirt road off the highway didn't go very far. I passed a house with a swimming pool in the back yard. A huge cement truck had somehow fallen into the pool and some men were trying to pull it out with a tractor. They were up to their ankles in mud. The weight of the truck had collapsed the walls of the pool and water had flooded out over the yard. I slowed down then kept on driving.

The road ended at an unpainted barn. There was a sign over the entrance: WORLD'S STRANGEST BABIES.

I parked the van and walked over. There were seven or eight people milling around. There was a little makeshift ticket office inside the door. The sign at the window was neatly drawn:

> WORLD'S STRANGEST BABIES
> A Non-Profit Education Show
> Admission
> Adults 75 cents
> Children 50 cents
> Chris Michael Christ, prop.

55
A Brief Conversation with Christ

I guessed the guy behind the window was Chris Michael Christ. He had a hare lip only partially hidden by a whispy moustache. He also had a whispy goatee. He looked sort of Oriental. He was wearing a dirty T-shirt bearing the slogan NO THANKS I GAVE AT THE ORIFICE. His fingernails were dirty.

'Jes' whan?' he said with a Deep South accent.

'Yes please.' I handed him a dollar and he gave me a quarter change, a ticket stub and a small neatly printed advertising flyer. The flyer indicated World's Strangest Babies was a touring show based in Gibsonton, Florida. I walked through into the dimly lit interior.

I don't even remember looking at the swimming pool disaster on the way back out five minutes later.

56
I Decide Not to Say Anything

'It's not very pleasant being left alone like this with two children in a foreign country,' said Joan. They hadn't been playing miniature golf after all. The place was closed. There was a sign over the door saying GONE OUT OF BUSINESS. I hadn't noticed it earlier when I left them there. They'd been standing there all this time, or actually sitting on a bench painted red, white and blue, outside the barred entrance to the miniature golf course. I guess they'd just sat there watching traffic go by.

'I didn't know if you were ever going to return.'

'You were worried about me?'

'I was worried about how I was going to get these kids home without a car.'

She didn't seem anxious to know where I'd been which was sort of a surprise. We got in the van and continued along the US 269. I decided not to tell her until she asked me. But as we approached Sandusky I realized she was never going to ask me. So I decided not to say anything. My resolve lasted less than a mile.

'Don't you want to know where I went?'

'Oh yeah, where did you go?'

I told her about the sign and how I wanted to check it out not for my own curiosity but just for the sake of the book, my writerly conscience. And how I was glad I followed my instinct not to take her and the kids.

'Was it that bad?'

'Oh, it was horrendous. There were about twenty card tables set up in the dimly lit interior of the barn. Each table had a little sign, a jar, and a lamp. The first one was ...'

'Don't tell me.'

'... called Elephant Nose Baby.'

'Don't tell me,' she said. 'I don't want to know.'

But I had to tell her anyway. I'm not saying I have to tell my wife absolutely everything but not telling her this would have made me feel uncomfortable. It would have been like keeping something from myself. Besides, the kids were listening at the back of the van. 'Come on, tell,' they kept saying.

What can I say? They were just ordinary babies. I sometimes collect mushrooms and you quite often come across a specimen that is deformed although still recognizable as a member of a certain species. You don't think anything about it. It's just there. Part of reality.

Elephant Nose Baby was a baby with a nose like an elephant's trunk. The baby was quite large, about six pounds. About as big as Jennifer when she was born. It was floating in some kind of preserving fluid.

There was no way of knowing how long it had been floating there. Maybe a month, maybe sixty years. It looked strangely alive, more than alive. It looked as if it were perfectly aware of the circumstances of its life and could tell what was going through my mind. Which was nothing really.

The trunk came down to the baby's chest. I wondered if the poor mother had seen it, what she thought. I was certain that most doctors' professional groups look askance at the trend towards natural childbirth techniques because of awkward situations like this which are probably not all that rare. Imagine the poor doctor. The mother lying there, ecstatic, waiting to be shown her baby.

Its eyes were open. Blue eyes. Curly blonde hair. Oh yes, perfectly formed genitalia. It was a male.

Frog Girl was dark-skinned, of African descent I suppose. A tiny pimple for a nose. A mouth that stretched from ear to ear. No chin at all. Eyes like golf balls staring out through the sugary light shed by the lamp. Perfect silence, stillness, and this unearthly light.

Cyclops had no nose at all. The eye was right where you would expect a cyclops' eye to be: smack dab in the middle of the forehead. No eyelid. It was set in and the flesh just crinkled around it. Under the eye were two nostrils the size of navels.

I was suddenly certain a race of these beings had lived at one time and died out. Their genes had obviously not been totally eradicated from the world's genepool. The genes are still there, here, waiting for an advantageous time to make their reappearance.

And maybe they will come back some day. All we need is someone with the good will to let a child like this live, and a world with enough tolerance to allow it to live without subjecting it to all sorts of cruelties.

Why not? Why are our formal assumptions so rigid? Perhaps they won't always be so.

Cyclops, Frog Girl, Elephant Nose Baby, I wish you'd been

allowed to live. Who knows what an incredible future died when you died?

58
In Flanders Fields the Palm Trees Blow

It seemed like any old day out on the road. But as we entered the heart of Sandusky we remembered it was Sunday morning. It was so quiet. And hot.

Sandusky was a beautiful little city. The streets were empty. The few people we saw seemed equally empty. Everywhere you looked there were traces of intelligent life but it seemed to have passed on to another planet.

The lack of intelligent life seemed to have something to do with Lake Erie lapping at a row of brightly coloured docks and pavilions a few blocks from the centre of town. One day a decade or two ago, perhaps around 1955, a mysterious underwater tornado appeared at the lakefront and sucked the soul of Sandusky into the deeps, never to reappear.

The poet Russell Seaworthy has a thing about palm trees growing in Southwestern Ontario. Whenever he visits the Caribbean or Hawaii he brings back palmetto seeds which he plants in various strategic points. He expects the first palm trees to start growing around the tip of Point Pelee. Maybe next year, maybe the year after. But it's inevitable. The tropics will return to Canada.

I don't know if Russell realizes this but palm trees can be found growing less than thirty miles south of Point Pelee, on the southern shore of Lake Erie, in the small city of Sandusky, Ohio.

The four of us wandered through the beautiful gardens surrounding the grand old courthouse. We took pictures of each other in front of the palm trees. Joan took cuttings of interesting looking plants in the hope she could get them across the border and be able to nurse them back into life at home. The children chased each other up the courthouse steps. Everything was so peaceful. We could hear the faint whistle of a popcorn vendor at the curbside.

Then we noticed a bronze plaque standing amid a bed of poppies. The plaque said the poppies had been grown from the seeds of the poppies of France in memory of the Erie County soldiers who had fallen in the Great War. The plaque also bore the words of the famous poem, 'In Flanders Fields.'

The poem was correctly attributed to Colonel John McRae. But there was no indication that McRae was a Canadian, from the city of Guelph, Ontario, and served in the Canadian Army. There was no indication the poem was anything but American. That would have been totally out of place on such a plaque. Let the people assume the writer was an American. McRae couldn't help it if he wasn't. Surely if he'd had a choice he would have been.

59

An Ordinary Mystical Experience and Two Mystical Experiences Involving Language

Also in the park was a life-size model of the famous Leaking Boot statue. It had been brought to Sandusky from Bavaria by a local druggist, Alfred W. Oates, in 1911.

For more than fifty years my grandfather owned a small china copy of this statue. It was about six inches tall. The boot was attached to the boy's hand by a tiny thread. When my grandfather died I came into possession of the charming little piece. It's sitting on a ledge not ten feet away from me now as I type. It appears to have been bought as a souvenir of Cleethorpes. A crest at the base bears the word 'Vigilantes.'

My grandfather was born in Sheffield, England, in 1900. We were good friends. When he died I felt a sense of absence. I kept looking back at myself and finding myself absent. My energy would go into whatever I was looking at and then it would look back expecting to see me standing there. But I wasn't there. I'd vanished.

The poet Steve McCaffery was also born in Sheffield, England, but in 1947. One night shortly after my grandfather's death Steve and I were discussing linguistics. I was telling him that at the beach one day I pointed at the water and asked the kids to tell me what I was pointing at.

'Water,' they said.

'No, that's not water. Water is a word. That's not a word.'

And suddenly the lake became something else. Our perception of it changed in a flash. It became all the things it has always been but it stopped being water. It became an element, one of the four Zoas. It became light. We looked at it with the innocence of a sandpiper or a painter.

Steve spoke of how writing provides for the absence of the writer. He spoke of how 'I' or 'you' are essentially matters of direction which map a landscape, the 'here' and the 'there.' And he spoke of what he called the 'it that is in everything.'

The conversation was quite exciting but it was past my bedtime and I found myself nodding off. I went to my room, crawled under the covers, and expected to fall off to sleep immediately. Surprisingly I didn't. Instead I became absent again. The mind's bubble burst and became a vacuum sucking in all the nameless, wordless aspects of the environment. I was merely a continuation of the 'it that is in everything.' I lay like that for hours, something warm

65

and soft enclosed in rough blankets on a bed in a small room on the shore of a great lake. I was simply the 'here.'

60
The Green Bikini

We left the park and walked along peaceful side streets leading to the waterfront. Everything seemed closed. The only signs of commercial life were the popcorn vendor and an old church beside the courthouse. Small groups of people walked silently in and out of the church, up and down the broad stone steps. The church was made from the same kind of stone as the courthouse.

We passed a drugstore that was open for business. Maybe it was Alfred W. Oates' drugstore. We went in.

There were two black children at the counter buying candy. They were dressed in their Sunday best. The clothes looked homemade but stylish. The kids had about four dollars and were stocking up on the most dreadful-looking candy concoctions.

The girl behind the counter was so beautiful she made my head feel light. She reminded me of a line from *The Master of Go*. 'A young poet coming down from Shiga Heights had taken note of the beautiful sisters at Jigokudani and passed on his impressions to me.'

Like all truly beautiful creatures she gave the impression of being unconcerned with her beauty, though not necessarily with herself. She was destined to spend the rest of her life in Sandusky, I felt, dressed in a white smock, her cream flesh slowly drying up and dying over the years. And then she would die like a mushroom in the heart of the forest, a once perfect mushroom, now bruised and misshapen, mourned only by those in her own little fairy ring.

A tall, elderly man was leaning over the counter, looking down at the girl and talking to her. I had the feeling he was sexually aroused. His voice had that familiar nervous, hoarse quality. He was about seventy-five years old.

'What are you going to do when you get out of here today?' he said.

It was a delicious moment for me. I knew I was about to hear the voice that went with that beautiful form. I couldn't help overhearing, especially when I turned my head sideways (to steal a line from Stephen Leacock). The pause was infinitessimal yet in that pause I became keen with anticipation. What would she say? What would her voice be like? Would it remind me of other beautiful women of my youth, women I'd succeeded in forgetting but whose memory would come back in a flash given the proper set of

cues? I prepared myself so that I might detect a hint of the attitude she was taking towards this old man who seemed to be on the make.

Whatever attitude she had assumed was subtly hidden. For all I knew in my innocence she'd been having a sneak affair with this old guy for years. She seemed to be amused, annoyed, bored, and slightly open to his advances all at the same time. All this was buried in a completely ordinary voice, not heavily accented, not particularly beautiful, not overly intelligent and not highly educated.

'Oh, I don't know', she said. 'Go down to the beach, maybe go over to Pelee.'

'What kind of bathing suit do you have?' The man was smiling. He was tall and thin, both elbows and knees bent in a strange combination of angles like in a Wyndham Lewis painting. He looked a bit like the Canadian poet Earle Birney.

'A bikini', she said.

'Hmm! A really small one?'

'Yeah.'

'What colour?'

'Green.'

'I'd love to see you in it.'

I was standing about ten feet away. I was pretending I was looking at a coin-operated machine which dispensed maps of Ohio, the Buckeye State. I decided it was rude to be listening and watching – even in such a subtle manner – so I approached the counter and asked the girl for change so I could buy a map.

I'll never know what I broke up. It might have been the cruellest thing I'd ever done in my life.

Joan was calling me over to the magazine display.

'Look at all this pornography', she said.

The kids were looking at the selection of hairdryers. Bruce was outside, his leash tangled around a parking meter. You could hear him barking.

61

Laughed at by a Family of Blacks

Sandusky is the terminus for the ferry which runs across Lake Erie between Leamington, Kingsville and Pelee Island. The Sandusky waterfront was brightly painted and well-maintained. This was a thing you notice in a lot of US cities. Old stuff is treated with a lot of respect just as a matter of course. You don't have to fight with obviously compromised city councillors to prevent old buildings from being torn down to make room for parking lots.

The Sandusky waterfront was like being back in the 1920s. The ferry departure area was under an old-fashioned pavilion with wooden supports and long painted benches. Someone was selling ice cream. A few people sat around with ferry tickets in their hands. Joan and the kids sat on a set of concrete steps leading down from the dock and down below the surface of the water. The steps had been built when the water level was lower. And the water level of Lake Erie has risen considerably since I was a kid. North shore beaches a hundred feet wide have been totally submerged in that time.

Everything looked old-fashioned but new in a curious way. There were hardly any people. It was sort of dream-like. It was like being in another era before the rot set in.

A large family of blacks drove slowly by in a black car. They pointed at me and laughed. I'm not just being paranoid. They really did. They were all looking at me and laughing their damned fool heads off. I couldn't figure out why. Then I thought it might have something to do with the brightly coloured African-styled shirt I was wearing. I forget what you call them. The kind that Canadian poet Dennis Lee wears all the time. Very comfortable. Joan's mother bought it for me. I think these shirts used to be quite popular with American blacks a decade or so back. That, combined with my lily white face (I can't help it) and the camera I was carrying, must have made me look ridiculous. But that was their problem, not mine. I didn't feel ridiculous. I didn't ask to be born white.

62
And the Streets Were Paved with Words

So much for Sandusky. We were driving southeast on the US 6, a highway that would take us into the mysterious heart of Cleveland. A few miles out of Sandusky we found ourselves trapped in a traffic jam. Thousands of cars were lined up waiting to get onto a sideroad leading north a few miles to Cedar Point where they have the world's largest movie screen. Remember Evelyn, the woman at Ned's Ledge?

'Sure you wouldn't like to see the world's largest movie screen, Joan?'

'No thank you.'

'They might be showing interesting Ohio travelogues.'

'No thank you.'

'They might be running a special documentary on the communist menace. Or a special preview of The Jack Spicer Story starring Archie Bunker and the Shorty Rogers All-Stars.'

'No thank you.'

'Imagine! A movie screen six storeys high! What a great country this is! The world's largest movie screen and the world's strangest babies!'

Joan's eyes sparkled. 'I'd rather see the world's strangest movie screen and the world's largest babies.'

We stopped at a roadside fresh fruit stand and bought baskets of peaches and plums. They were terrible. They tasted as if chemical flavouring had been added. 'We should take these back and tell them to shove it,' said Joan. But we didn't. In fact we eventually ate them all ourselves. Grumbling with every bite.

We stopped at a gas station. 'Where ya headin'?' said the guy.

'East,' I said. 'For years we've been visiting the Canadian side of Lake Erie and we just got a little curious about what this side looked like.'

The guy smiled weakly. He looked bored, as if I'd told him a little more than he really wanted to know. If I wanted to be an entertainer I should go on television, he seemed to be saying.

Passing through the town of Huron, Joan spotted an interesting looking place to spend some money. It was the Wileswood Country Store, a little bit of Americana, a white clapboard house in the nineteenth-century style with Old Glory blowing in the wind on top of a fifty-foot-high flagstaff. A black eagle plaque was nailed above the door. 'Nothing unpatriotic about us,' the tableau seemed to be saying.

I didn't feel like going in. It seemed a little depressing. So I took Bruce for a little walk. We went over to the Texaco station on the corner. It was on a v-shaped lot wedged into a fork in the road. The sign on the washroom said CUSTOMERS ONLY. Well, I'm a customer. I buy gas quite often as well as a lot of other things although not here.

The door was locked. I walked around the front with the dog. There was a greasy-looking, mean-looking, tattooed fellow about fifty-four years old sitting there looking as if he needed a drink in the worst way. I asked him politely for the key to the men's room.

He pointed at little Bruce. In case I haven't mentioned it already Bruce was a West Highland white terrier. You'll read a lot more about him in *A Trip around Lake Huron*.

'He's not a man,' the guy said.

Very perceptive of you, I thought. 'No, I guess he's not, but I am,' I said.

'You can just leave him somewhere. I'm not having him going in there pissing all over the floor I just mopped up.'

I couldn't believe this guy. 'I got a truck around the corner with an empty gas tank,' I said. 'It needs oil. And it needs a new set of spark plugs. You just missed out on a nice big sale. This dog is less **69** likely to piss on the floor than you are by the looks of you. Where's the next gas station?'

The guy was about as perturbed as if I'd shot him with an empty water pistol. He coughed up a bit of phlegm and scored a direct hit on the waste-paper basket. The floor of the station was pretty clean. The phlegm dripped slowly down the inside of the basket.

'You can go to any gas station you want,' he said. 'I've always heard tell this here's a free country. And the best part of it is *he'* – he pointed at poor little Bruce who was wagging his tail at the guy – 'ain't goin' in there.'

'Come on, Bruce,' I said. We walked away. I thought of pulling in with my van, asking for him to fill it up, then driving away just as he went to remove the gas cap. But then I thought he might take off after us in his car and shoot us. Maybe that's what happened to that motorcyclist from Hamilton who was found shot to death on the side of an Ohio road on his way back from Florida.

63

Fat

We passed through Ruggles Beach and Beulah Beach. Ah, if only William Blake were here! Then we stopped at Vermilion, which, according to a roadside sign, was 'named after the red clay Indians used for paint.' We looked at a marine museum over-looking the lake. The Frank Lloyd Wright architecture was nice but we didn't feel like going in. I took a picture of the beach with Lake Erie sparkling in the background. The picture showed people sunbathing on the sand, swimming in the lake, a few sails out there on the horizon, and in the foreground an enormously fat man fully dressed and framed between two thin trees.

'There sure are a lot of fat people in this country,' said Joan. 'Everywhere you turn – fatties. The United Fatties of America.'

It was true that fat seems to have a different meaning in this country. You're simply not a real man unless you have a big fat gut. The attitude towards fat is only noticeable in the more rural areas, and is particularly noticeable in the southern states. It seems to be a redneck phenomenon. A huge gut is a sign of success.

This attitude towards fat is betrayed by the fact that young men who haven't yet developed a lot of fat on their bellies adopt the manner of walking generally associated with really fat men. Even though they're thin, they waddle and hold their arms out semi-horizontally like a grossly obese person. It's a dead give-away. Just as it's obvious that a guy with sideburns, sunglasses and a sneer is an Elvis Presley fan, it's obvious that a thin guy who waddles with his arms held out semi-horizontally at his side is an admirer of fat Georgia sheriffs.

We'd been warned to avoid Lorain because of the ugly steel mills. I think it was Ned of Ned's Ledge who warned us. But I thought that was kind of hypocritical of him. His car was made of steel, the high school where he works is built on steel beams. How can he talk disparagingly of the city where this steel is produced, a city where thousands of men give their lives to its production?

Besides, I liked what I saw of Lorain. There were millions of acres of railway yards straddling the Black River which empties into Lake Erie at this point. And the air around Lorain seemed relatively clean, much cleaner than in the lower east side of Hamilton, Ontario, where the entire McFadden family used to live until they scraped up enough money to move up the Mountain.

But Lorain was a nice little place. It made me feel warm inside. I'll always have a soft spot for densely industrial architecture. The incredible beauty of steel mills, all the more beautiful because it wasn't intended to be and is not widely considered to be. There's something about a dusty, barbed-wire, weed-filled lot surrounding a steel warehouse that makes me think of childhood and home.

64
Childhood and Home

We kept going along US 6 and soon found ourselves heading through sedate lakeside Cleveland suburbs with names like Sheffield Lake, Avon Lake, Bay Village, Rocky River and Lakewood. Each had originally been a town in its own right and each had its own brownbrick 1910ish water filtration plant. The homes along the route were large and well-built but dull in style, not very imaginatively designed. Yet each had a black eagle nailed over the entrance to the garage, just above the basketball hoop. And there were a lot of US flags flying.

One could imagine Mickey Rooney – or some of the characters he played in his early films – growing up here. But the original families seemed to have moved out. The lakefront area west of Cleveland seems to have been taken over by ordinary middle-aged lawyers.

65
Mickey Rooney

66

Edgewater Park

After spending three hours driving through the western suburbs we passed a small sign saying CLEVELAND CITY LIMIT. Then we passed a large lakeside park on the left.

This was Edgewater Park. We decided to stop and let the kids have a swim if the water seemed okay and maybe a picnic.

We parked in the parking lot overlooked by a lovely old Persian-style pavilion suitably rundown. The park was built on a forty-foot bluff at the bottom of which was a wide sandy beach. You could climb down and swim. There were people frolicking in the surf and sunning on the sand.

I went through the pavilion. They sold soft drinks and ice cream and potato chips. There were two large change rooms and toilets. There was a big hole the size of a fist in the wall of the men's washroom. Through the hole you had a perfect view of the women's washroom. I looked through and saw Joan looking back.

I sat on a bench overlooking the lake. Some tiny blackflies, midges, or no-see-ums nipped at my ankles as if I weren't there. Or at least as if the rest of me weren't there. I didn't think such animals wandered this far south. It got so bad that when a moth landed on my left elbow I expected it to bite me and I jerked my arm to frighten it off.

When I wandered back to the car a couple of black guys in their early twenties or maybe even in their teens were talking to Joan. 'Can you help them fix their car, Dave?' she said. Their battery was dead. Their rusty old heap was even worse than mine.

'We got cables', said one of them. He was wearing a nice black satin shirt with a picture of a beautiful black woman on the back.

They pulled the cables out of the trunk and we hooked them up. I started my car and theirs started right away.

As they were putting away the cables the guy with the shirt, Chico, handed me a joint. 'You get high?' he said.

'No thanks. You keep it.'

'I just wanna give you a little gift for helpin' us, man.'

'Do you want a joint, Joan?' I said. She was sitting on the blanket.

'No thanks, dear.'

'Sorry', I said to Chico.

'Hey, well thanks a lot anyway', he said. The two of them drove off. They'd be back later.

I took some pictures of the Cleveland skyline from the park. There were ships entering the wide mouth of the Cuyahoga River which was lined with steel mills, and the highlight of the skyline was the Terminal Tower building, a 1920ish skyscraper billed as the tallest building in all of Ohio. It was quite a lovely, human skyline fronted by a long, curved beach and a small baseball diamond with bleachers, the steelmills not belching out smoke the way they do in Canada, and the buildings of the city itself faint in the distance.

We spread a blanket on the grass under some trees in front of the pavilion and Joan made sandwiches. I took the kids into the pavilion so they could change into their swimsuits. When we returned the black guys were back talking to Joan. They asked her if all that food was just for us. Then when I approached they told me they'd borrowed a new battery and the car was working fine now.

'It's nice you've got such close friends you can borrow a battery just like that,' I said. I love to pretend I'm naive, even more naive than I really am.

They looked at each other, trying not to laugh. I smiled. They left. But they'd be back.

After we ate our sandwiches and drank some tea we walked down to the beach. The water was fairly disagreeable-looking close in to the shore but it became clean after you waded out for about ten feet through the muck. It wasn't as bad really as the Canadian side around Turkey Point and places like that. And there weren't any dead fish along the shore. Of course the city probably kept the beach clean daily during the summer. And there were quite a few lifeguards, something you rarely see on Canadian beaches.

So the kids went splashing through the scum. Bruce started tugging at his leash. He'd seen a small brown dog nearby, being held on a leash by a black man sitting on the sand.

'Is your dog's name Rusty by any chance?'

'No. She's Mizz,' he said. 'Aren't you, girl?'

The lifeguards started yelling back and forth to each other. They were on wooden towers about fifty feet apart. They seemed to be yelling in some kind of code.

The kids finally came out and we started walking slowly up the bluff to the car. The same black guys caught up with us again. They said we shouldn't have let our kids swim in that awful water.

'They used to post it but they just can't keep the people out,' said one of them, not Chico, the other one. They walked with us back to the car, then got in their own and took off.

At one point I asked them how come the lifeguards were white and the guys picking up the garbage were black, and how come when you go into a restaurant it's always the waitress is white and the cook is black.

'That's just the way it is,' said Chico. 'It ain't never going to change.'

68

We Vow to Return to Cleveland

If we'd gone south on the US 42 from Edgewater Park for a couple of miles we could have visited the famous Cleveland Zoo but at the time we couldn't find the zoo marked on our map of the city and if there were any signs on the road we missed them. Besides, it was getting rather late in the afternoon and Joan wanted to get through Cleveland and settled in a campsite before dark. If we'd chosen to drive along the Alternate 6 instead of the US 6 we might have seen signs pointing to the zoo and as it turned out we might have camped in any one of a number of campgrounds in the huge Metropolitan Cleveland park system that circles the city. But then we probably never would have met the McFaddens, the other McFaddens that is, the McFadden family of Sheraton Heights.

So we followed the US 6 over the Cuyahoga River which achieved considerable fame a few years back when it caught fire. We drove past Municipal Stadium, the home of the Cleveland Indians and the Cleveland Browns, then switched on to the US 20 which becomes Euclid Avenue.

It was Sunday afternoon in Cleveland and there was little traffic. We passed right by the Terminal Tower building I'd photographed in the distance from Edgewater Park, then drove around the Soldiers and Sailors Monument, a spectacular nineteenth-century sculpture located in the middle of a traffic circle which appeared to mark the central point of the city. It made me think of Hart Crane. In fact the whole central section of the city seems to have changed little since his day, and it has been well-maintained. I sound like a used car salesman.

Euclid Avenue runs northeast from the traffic circle and parallels the lakeshore at a distance of about two miles right out of the city, into the suburbs and eventually into the rural flatlands of the northeastern part of the state.

There were a lot of stores with iron gates tightly locked to prevent burglaries, with black people standing around outside looking slightly humiliated. Further out we passed a beautiful series of buildings including the Cleveland Art Museum, the Institute of Art, the Institute of Music, the Fine Arts Garden, the

74 Garden Centre, the Natural History Museum, the Planetarium, the Western Reserve Historical Society and so on, all surrounded by a series of parks and winding roads. We drove around and around gawking at the beautiful architecture and vowed to come back some day when we had some time to spend.

A few more miles and we were into the ghastly suburbs.

Joan was napping in the back seat. Alison was up front with me. As we drove along we saw what looked like sheets of water lying ahead of us on the road, the images of approaching cars reflected in the shimmering mirrors.

69
I Love That
Kind of Moon

'I love those optical illusions', said Alison.

'Why?'

'Because they remind me of summer.'

'I know.'

An earlier scene flashed into my mind. I was driving home late at night and Alison was asleep in the back seat. She was about two years old. In the western sky, just skimming the treetops, was a crescent moon, a thin fingernail of a moon so slight it was easy to miss.

As I carried Alison in from the car, thinking she was sleeping, I suddenly heard her voice.

'Oh, look at that moon', she cried. 'I love that kind of moon.'

Another watery mirage appeared on the road in front of us. Alison and I looked at each other and giggled. It was strange. We'd both seen something that wasn't there and it gave us a special bond all over again.

'What causes those optical illusions?' she said.

'You can look it up in the encyclopedia when we get home. I don't really know.'

It was the 201st birthday of the universe, at least that's what you'd almost think it was as we drove into Fairport Harbour on the Lake Erie shore. There were flags everywhere. People were sitting on their verandahs waving flags and staring hypnotically into space. Others were milling along the streets in the general direction of the lakefront.

70
A Festive
Atmosphere

It was a warm evening. The road began dipping down towards the beach. Then we could see the amusement park. There was a ferris wheel, rides, carousels, a midway and thousands of people swarming in and out, each with an American flag in his or her hand. You could tell they weren't ants because they were colourfully dressed.

'The kids haven't noticed the rides,' said Joan, quietly. 'Let's get out of here.'

I turned right. The kids were looking out the other window. They were staring at the people sitting on their verandahs with patriotic embalming fluid pumping through their veins. It was Sunday evening.

71

Sex in Ohio

We drove north on the US 44 towards the lake. There was something called Headlands State Beach Park marked on the map. But when we got there there was a sign saying NO OVERNIGHT CAMPING. People were packing up their cars and heading home after a hard day of swimming and picnicking. Some people were lying on their bellies on blankets under the trees. They were not tourists. They were just local people with the day off. We examined each person carefully from a discreet distance as we drove slowly by. We knew we'd never see any of them ever again.

We drove through an industrial dock area where an old Great Lakes steamer was being loaded with slag. A byproduct of the steelmaking process, for years slag was considered useless except as landfill in harbours, to destroy waterbasins and provide more useable industrial land. But now it's used in building highways, ground up fine and mixed with asphalt.

We stopped at a traffic signal in a town called Grand River. Joan said something funny, I forget what it was, and I smiled. As I smiled I looked out the window at a car parked across the street. There was a beautiful woman behind the wheel. She was looking at me. I guess she thought I was smiling at her because she smiled right back. She looked like someone I'd seen on the cover of *Oui*, and maybe she was. After all, this was the United States. She had a pretty smile.

'Let's see now,' I thought to myself. 'Where can I leave Joan and the kids?' Then I erased the thought, a spiritual sacrifice towards unknown but certainly glorious ends. We were still looking at each other and smiling merrily when the light turned green.

'The light's green,' said Joan.

'All right, all right,' I said, driving off. Cursing my miserable fate. Looking back. Hoping she would follow us and tap on my window at 3 AM in the next camping site.

A little further on we passed a young man walking along the side of the road. He had his shirt off. He was well-built and well-tanned. He had a perfect body like Russell Seaworthy. We were driving fairly slowly at the time and I noticed Joan giving him as thorough an examination as she could under the circumstances.

'Do you want me to let you out?' I said.

'What do you mean?' exclaimed Joan, angry at my sarcasm and at the same time pleased with my jealousy. She hadn't noticed the little romantic interlude at the stoplight.

'If I let you out you could go back and examine him even more closely.'

'Wait a minute. If there was a woman walking along the street with no shirt on you'd look at her too.'

'It's not the same thing.'

'Yes it is.'

We bypassed Painesville and got onto the US 20 heading east. 'What a name for a town,' said Joan. Little did we know we'd be back the next day.

72
Aspirin Consumption in Painesville, Ohio

'What's in a name?'

'I don't know. What *is* in a name?' said Joan.

'I wonder if the people of Painesville consume more aspirins per capita than people in other American towns of similar size.'

Joan didn't answer.

'Well?'

'Are you *asking* me?'

'Yes.'

'How would *I* know?'

'Well, what do you *think*?'

She didn't answer.

'Well?'

'I'm *think*ing, I'm *think*ing.'

'I think they probably would, Daddy,' said Alison.

'Why would they?'

'I know,' said Joan, anxious not to be outsmarted by her kid.

'Why?'

'Because it would be a pain living in Painesville.'

'What about you, Jenny, what do *you* think?'

'Sh! She's sleeping, Dad.'

'Oh.'

We kept driving. I could tell they were still thinking about Painesville. 'I was once talking to a woman named Mrs. Payne, who was a yoga teacher,' I said. 'I told her I thought that was an unusual name for a yoga teacher. She seemed a little put out and said, "It's a perfectly normal name."'

73

The Story of O

'What two things do Ontario and Ohio have in common?'

'Lake Erie?' said Alison.

'Good but that's not it. *Two* things.'

'The ferry and the lake?' said Jennifer.

'Good but that's still not what I'm thinking of.'

'They both begin with an O and they both end with an O?'

'Joan, you're brilliant!'

'Was that it, Daddy?' said Alison.

'Yeah, that was it.'

'Gee, Mommy. You're smart.'

Traffic on the US 20 was getting heavy. I wondered what was being said in other cars.

74

Miracle on US 20

We were driving east along the US 20. I had my left foot propped up on the dashboard in my favourite driving position. I was flicking my eyes back and forth between the road and the Rand McNally map of Ohio I bought for four quarters in that drugstore in Sandusky. 'Use this map to plan the shortest route', it said. 'Please SLOW down. It will save lives as well as gasoline.' We were looking for a place to camp for the night.

There was a Chevy van passing us on the left. A little girl was looking out the back seat window at our van. I smiled at her and winked.

There didn't seem to be much in the way of campgrounds in this area. It certainly wasn't prime tourist territory like the Port Clinton-Marblehead area where we'd camped the night before. Gad, had that only been last night?

At a town called Perry the US 20 decreased from four lanes and a median to an old-style two-lane highway. We slowed down appropriately.

The map showed a little dot called North Skylark a few miles further along the 20. From there a faint black line marked 520 went a mile or two north to a place called Skylark-on-the-Lake. Then it made a sharp right turn, became the 530 and ran along the lake, hugging the shore past Ashtabula and all the way to the Pennsylvania border at which point it turned south into the 20 again.

'What do you think, Joan?' I said. 'Will there be a greater chance of finding a campsite along this highway or along the lakeshore road?'

'Let's try the lakeshore road,' said Joan, decisively.

So we went through the traffic light at North Skylark and pulled into a vacant supermarket parking lot to turn around to go up the 520. The bloody parking lot wasn't paved. We hit a rut and bounced so hard we almost hit our heads on the roof. As we slowed down and began driving out the exit a Chevy van pulled up. The driver, a narrow-faced man with a full beard, looked at me sternly.

I braked to a halt.

'Where you from?' he said.

'Canada', I said.

He looked at me as though I was stupid. 'I *see* you got Ontario plates. I mean what part of Ontario?'

'Hamilton.'

'Oh, we have some relatives used to live in Mount Hope but they moved to Niagara-on-the-Lake.'

'That's quite near us', I exclaimed.

He looked at me again that way. 'I know', he said. He smiled at his wife. 'Where ya headin'?'

I checked the map. 'We're heading up the 520 to the lake. We're looking for a campsite.'

'We live up the 520', he said. 'Why don't you follow me home and we'll have a cup of tea and we'll phone around looking for a campsite?'

'Okay', I said, a little nervously. I just knew it was going to be more than a cup of tea.

'Follow me', he said. 'It's not far.'

'Did you know there was a town in Ohio called Delightful?' I asked Joan as we followed the Chevy van north.

'Where?' said Joan.

'In Ohio', I said.

'Yeah, but where in Ohio?'

'About fifty miles south of here on the outskirts of Warren which is on the outskirts of Youngstown.'

'Dave, this is crazy.'

'I know.'

'What if he's a crazy man and wants to shoot us?'

'I don't know. You shouldn't be prejudiced against him just because he's an American. Murders happen in Canada too you know.'

'I know. But this would never happen in Canada.'

'Listen. He's got his wife there and the little kids in the back. He's got relatives in Canada. They're an average family just like us.' The kids were waving at us out their back window. 'Look at that. They're probably just lonely. They want someone to talk to.

75
This Would Never Happen in Canada

Maybe there are no children in their neighbourhood and they want someone for their kids to play with.'

76
Besides, It'll Look Good in the Book

'Besides,' I said.

'Besides what?' said Joan.

'It'll look good in the book.'

'Ah, they'll never believe you. They'll think you made it up.'

'Oh, come on, Joan. It's not *that* unusual.'

'No, I guess it's not. Not yet anyway.'

The Chevy van turned left onto a tree-lined suburban street. We followed.

'You can help me, you know,' I said.

'How?'

'By observing everything that happens and listening to everything they say so we can write it all down as soon as we leave.' They say Malcolm Lowry's wife wrote most of *Under the Volcano*.

'Maybe they'll want us to stay the night.'

'Maybe. They'll probably want to check us out first over tea. They might be scared too.'

'Yeah,' said Joan. 'But we didn't ask them. And they probably have guns in their house. Loaded guns. Maybe even in their car. You know Americans. You don't fool around with them.'

'I know, I know.'

'And Dave?'

'Yeah?'

'Don't get into any fights, okay?'

'Okay, okay.'

'Agree with everything he says, okay?'

'Okay.'

'No matter what he says, okay?'

'Okay.'

'Promise?'

'I promise.'

77
Joan Gets Drunk

On the Rand McNally map of Ohio, Cleveland is an orange blob in the shape of an American eagle, its wings outspread, its head facing down and its beak open. The town of Skylark looks as if it's about to be swallowed.

We were led into the driveway of a small house with a large garage. No room to put us up for the night, I noted. No basement for instance. We had a slightly smaller house but it had a basement, and no garage. And suddenly there we were: a typical

Canadian family from the north side of Lake Erie facing a typical American family from the south side of Lake Erie.

And then I noticed their name on a sign stuck in the lawn. There were two little painted figures, a boy and a girl, holding up this sign bearing the family name. I couldn't believe it. The name was the same as ours: MCFADDEN.

'Holy Christ, that's not your name is it?'

'Yes it is', said the guy, again giving me that look.

'That's my name too.' I was opening my wallet to show him my driver's licence.

'I believe you, I believe you', he said.

'Same spelling too', I said.

'What a coincidence', he said, calmly.

'I'd just die if your first name was the same as mine', I said.

'What's yours?' he said, smiling.

'It starts with a D.'

'So does mine', he said.

'Oh, no. It couldn't be. David?'

'No. Donald.'

'Phew. That was close.'

It had been a hot day and the kids were getting into their bathing suits and hopping into the backyard pool. Lamont was seven and his hobby was pulling down girls' pants. Tania was ten and had the same favourite rock and roll band as my kids: Kiss.

The adults sat around the kitchen table sipping tea and swapping life stories.

After her third cup of tea Joan started in on the beer and really started to unwind. 'Dave's a writer and he's writing a story about this trip', she blurted out. 'No one who reads the book is going to believe this part.'

Don's expression didn't change. 'When it comes out I'll be the first one to buy it', he said, unsmilingly. He was a serious person.

'Why don't you camp in our driveway tonight?' said Chloris, Don's wife, a rather large woman about thirty. She looked like a younger version of the famous Canadian novelist Margaret Laurence, and she spoke with a Scottish accent. She'd met Don when he was in the US Navy stationed in Scotland. Don had been born in Scotland too, but came to the US with his family when he was five. He quit high school to join the navy.

'I thought I was being really smart', he said. 'Now I know better.'

He had a polar bear skin on the living room floor. It was from a small bear. It must have been a mere cub when it was killed. It

78
A Lot of Good Men Died in Vietnam

came from Iceland. Don had served in Vietnam during the sixties.

'I saw a lot of good men killed in that war,' he said. His eyes filled with tears. 'I'd prefer not to talk about it.' My heart went out to him. I understood completely. They'd trusted their leaders. They were sacrificing their lives for something they thought was beautiful. And now the awful truth was out. If they had only won the war.

79

Americans Like to Brag about Their Dogs

Behind the swimming pool was a pen with two dogs in it, vicious looking dogs but really quite gentle. They were chained.

'Why do you keep them chained when they're already inside the pen?' said Joan.

'Because that one is the world's best climber and this one is the world's best tunnel digger,' said Don.

Then Tania came over.

'See this dog?' she said. 'If there was a contest for climbing he'd win it. And the other one would win any contest for digging holes.'

Then Chloris came over.

'These are really remarkable dogs,' she said. 'Bobby here could climb Mount Everest and Ralph could dig a tunnel out of San Quentin Penitentiary.'

80

How Do You Like Your Steaks?

It was getting late. Chloris put her kids to bed and Joan and I got our kids settled down in the van.

'You're right, Joan,' I said. 'Nobody's gonna believe this.'

'What made you change your mind?'

'Their name. It's the same as ours. Now that is a thousand times more incredible than simply getting picked up by them.'

The kids fell asleep quickly. It was all the swimming.

The four adults were sitting at the kitchen table when Chloris got up and started doing something at the microwave oven. Don started telling us about how their old oven had exploded one day and the whole kitchen was engulfed in flames. With the insurance settlement and a little cheating they managed to get a $2,000 microwave unit out of the deal.

Chloris' voice suddenly rang out.

'How do you like your steaks?'

'Well done,' said Joan, delightedly, without hesitation.

'None for me, thanks, I'm a vegetarian,' said I.

'No he's not, he's just fooling,' said Joan.

'Yeah, I was just fooling. I'll have mine well done too.'

82   'That's another coincidence for your book,' said Don. 'We like ours well done too.' He was opening a bottle of California burgundy.

I could have killed Joan for telling them I was writing a book. I gave her a menacing look.

'I think Dave's mad at me,' she blurted out, 'because I told you about the book he was writing.'

They all looked at me.

'Heh, heh,' I said. 'Bad luck to talk about a book before it's written. You know?'

By the time we were finished the meal Joan who normally drinks next to nothing was getting pretty unwound on all that beer and wine. But Don was even more unwound.

'Ready for a swim?' he said.

'I don't have a suit with me,' said Joan.

'Neither do I,' said I. I was expecting them to suggest skinny-dipping but then I noticed the neighbours' windows overlooked the pool. So skinny-dipping was pretty well ruled out.

'I can lend you one,' Chloris said to Joan.

'Okay!' said Joan, brightly.

That was a little strange. Joan is usually shy about appearing in a swimsuit. Further, she's pretty small and would swim in any suit of Chloris'.

'And I've got a pair of denim cut-offs that would fit *you*,' said Don.

'Okay,' I said.

But before we changed Don took me into the garage to show me his Honda 350. 'It's my pride and joy,' he said. He said it was no good on the highway because of the low gear ratios so he couldn't take it back and forth to work. He worked as a welder in a Towmotor plant in Painesville.

'It'll only do about fifty on the highway. But it's really good around town. Nothing will beat it at a stoplight. And it's a good trail bike. Riding along country roads, lanes, nature trails, through the woods.'

He started it up. The roar was deafening. Anyone who would ride one of those through the woods or along nature trails has got to be pretty insensitive to nature, I thought. But then again we all must be pretty insensitive to nature or we wouldn't be where we are today. On the brink of extinction.

I think he was half-expecting me to ask him if I could take it for a spin.

82
Most Americans Look like Someone Famous

We went out into the driveway. I wanted to make sure the kids were okay and to lock the doors just in case. With Joan half-pissed I had to be particularly responsible.

Across the street a woman was taking her dogs out for a leak. 'Hey Tinker Bell!' called out Don. 'Tinker Bell!'

She walked over, cautiously. The dogs started running in huge circles around her. One was a semi-collie, the other a small white poodlish creature. They were really excited.

'Is the Ogre asleep?' said Don.

'Yeah, at last!' said Tinker Bell. She was really short, about four-foot-nine, with breasts a little too large for her size. She had an unusual face, soft and not unattractive. She was aptly named.

'Wanna come in for a swim?' said Don. I just stood there watching as if I had become invisible.

'Is it safe?' she said.

'Of course it's safe.'

'It wasn't last time.'

'Go get your suit.'

It didn't occur to me to ask about the Ogre or the reference to safety. I just wanted to relax and see what happened. I just hoped the Ogre didn't come over with a .38-calibre revolver when he found out his wife had slipped out on him again in the middle of the night.

Most Americans look like somebody famous, I thought. But I never saw any movie star or rock star or television star who looked like Tinker Bell. She was a true original as far as the unusualness of her face was concerned. I thought maybe she should go to Hollywood.

In fact it began to occur to me that most Americans are resentful of not being rich and famous. They watch TV and go to the movies to feed their jealousy. That's it. I'm sure. It explains everything. Think about it. Quick, before it goes away!

83
The Arrows of Your Heart

Joan was the first one in the pool. I think she jumped in first because she was so shy in the bathing suit Chloris had lent her. It was too big for her and every time she moved her breasts were revealed in all their occult grandeur. She called out to me once she got in.

'How's the water?' I said.

'Beautiful. But Dave?'

'Yes?'

'Will you get me a string for this bathing suit? It's too big for me.'

Chloris gave me a shoe lace and I tossed it in the pool for Joan. I immediately felt stupid. It was the sort of thing a man who's been married too long would do.

'Let me', said Don, diving in and picking up the string from the surface of the water.

He laced it through the suit and took up the slack and then tied it gently around Joan's neck. I could see Joan blushing in the moonlight.

Then Chloris and Tinker Bell and I jumped in the pool under the soft summer sky of Ohio in a huge land of endless cities and towns and villages and railway stations and post offices fading away in any direction you choose to send the arrows of your heart. Maybe that's why most Americans look so bored.

I built a little fire in the back yard with bricks to shelter it from the night breezes.

'Look at that', said Don. 'He's really got a good fire going'.

I was proud. Only one match too.

We dried off and warmed up around the fire, our toes almost touching. In the pool Don kept grabbing the three women by the ankles, around the waist and so on, and throwing them into the air and catching them and chasing after them and swimming up to them underwater and scaring them and all that stuff. But I just dogpaddled around keeping out of their way. I guess they figured I was a square.

Things really quietened down after that. We went in the house and sat at the kitchen table. Don got out more beer. Chloris got out her stamp albums. She had a nice collection. When Don saw how interested I was he knew for sure he had a square on his hands. Stamp collections?

Chloris had stamps from all over the world. Tinker Bell on the other hand was into macramé. She couldn't get over our names being the same.

'Hey!' she said. 'McFadden, McFadden, and McRamé'.

'Ohh!' said everyone.

It was very nostalgic looking through Chloris's stamp albums from her childhood. I'd had many of the same stamps when I was a kid.

'See that one?' she said.

'Yes?'

'That's worth $300'.

'Oh no', I cried. 'I had dozens of them when I was a kid but they all got tossed out'.

84

Chloris Gets Out Her Stamp Collection

'Are you sure this isn't *Fernwood*, Ohio?' Joan kept saying. She was referring to a television series about some middleclass suburban goofballs. It was really popular that year. It was called *Mary Hartman, Mary Hartman*.

'If you say that once more I'll kill you,' said Chloris.

She sounded as if she meant it.

85

A Serious Discussion about the Environment

Don and I were two responsible adult male humans having a serious discussion about water quality.

'How does this side of the lake compare with the other side?' said Don.

'There aren't as many dead fish on the beaches over here,' I said.

'Yeah. After the Cuyahoga River caught fire a couple of years ago everyone panicked and they got started on a clean-up campaign.'

'It might have something to do with the prevailing winds as well,' I added.

'Yeah,' said Don. 'I guess so.'

86

We Get Out of the Pool Just in Time

We were continuing our serious talk when there was an immense flash of lightning, a bolt of thunder and it started to rain like mad.

'We got out of the pool just in time,' I said.

'Yeah,' said Don. 'Otherwise we would have got all wet.'

'And just think,' said Joan. 'The moon was shining not five minutes ago.'

'Yeah. Just think.'

'Gee,' said Tinker Bell. 'It's raining cats and dogs.'

'They look like drops of water to me,' said Don.

87

The Americans Land on the Moon

We took off our wet bathing suits and put on dry clothing. The women were sitting at the kitchen table. Don was lying down on one of the two sofas in the living room. He told me to lie down on the other one. 'Go ahead, it's comfortable,' he said. It was about two-thirty in the morning.

Don started telling me about his job, how he works steady nights. This was his night off. He said he liked steady nights because there was less stress, you could goof off more, there were no bosses snooping around, there was less traffic to fight going to and from work, and you could sleep any time you wanted during the day or early evening. It was nice to walk around during the day when everyone else was at work. And on top of that you got paid more for working nights.

'I know all that,' I said. 'I worked steady nights for seven years.'

I told him about the painter John Boyle who couldn't get any work done for three months after he left his teaching job to become a fulltime artist. All he wanted to do was experience the joy of walking around town during the day when everyone else was working. 'That was in St. Catharines,' I said. 'It's not the same in Hamilton. Almost everyone's a shiftworker there.'

He started telling me about how sick little Lamont was when he was first born. 'After a while I stopped hoping he would live,' he said. 'I just gave up on him.' Tears came into his eyes. 'He's pretty good now but he still gets terrible bouts of bronchitis. Did you see him shivering when he came out of the water?'

I did notice that, and that he was the only one of the four kids shivering. He wrapped himself up in the largest blanket, the one commemorating the manned landing on the moon. The one with the American flag sticking out of a yellow crater and the words about man and mankind. I was never good at remembering unforgettable quotes.

Then Don started telling me how sick *he* was. The story about little Lamont was just a warm-up. I didn't know what to think. It sounded serious. He showed me the scar from his kidney operation. One kidney had been removed. The other was in bad shape. He had to go back into the hospital in a month.

88
Moving to Utah

'It's an incurable disease with a name this long,' he said. He took another slug of beer.

'Wouldn't it be better if you cut down on the beer?'

'If the doctors told me cutting down on beer would help I'd quit drinking immediately. But if I'm going to have a short life I'm going to enjoy it.'

I didn't want to pump him on it although I had a feeling he wanted me to. He looked kind of grey. I asked him about dialysis. He said he couldn't go on it. I didn't ask him why.

Joan later theorized that he was dying and that's why Chloris had indulged his little whim to invite us home. Chloris had made it clear in small ways that it had been his idea totally.

And yet Don talked about quitting his job and moving with his family to Utah. Or maybe to New Zealand. He really wanted to move to San Francisco but Chloris wouldn't hear of it. 'I don't relish living in the earthquake zone', she said. New Zealand was more to her liking.

Don was a Republican and hated the current US President, Jimmy Carter. He was annoyed about the cancellation of the plans to build some new American bomber. It was big in the news all that summer. 'I have a feeling he's going to start another war, the biggest of all time. And if he does you're going to have another neighbour', he said. Meaning himself.

89
Greasy Little Wop

I told Don how the black family in the car pointed at me and laughed as I was standing on a street corner in Sandusky on a warm Sunday afternoon in my African-style shirt.

'You're lucky they just pointed at you. You're lucky they didn't point a gun at you. You're lucky they didn't shoot you.'

'Aw, come on. Is it really that bad?'

'You better believe it, baby.'

'But was it my shirt they were laughing at or was it something else?'

'What were you doing?'

'Just standing there with a camera in my hand.'

'Could have been the shirt.'

'It wasn't really African anyway,' said Joan. 'It was made in Pakistan.'

'There's good and bad in every race', Don was saying. 'I work with a lot of black guys. Some really great guys as far as I'm concerned. They ask me how I liked *Roots,* the television series? I tell them I liked it but it was kind of one-sided. We were all slaves at one time. The blacks had it a heck of a lot better than my ancestors at the hands of the Romans. They killed us whenever they felt like it. We were dirt cheap. When they killed one of us another was right there. They didn't have to import us all the way across the sea from Africa.'

'You got a point there', I said. I told him about our trip through Cleveland.

'You could have been in a lot of trouble if you'd got out of your car', he said. He looked at me with his serious blue eyes, a light shade of blue, almost white, like Paul Newman's. 'A Canadian is easy picking for them. They'd take you for all you're worth and if that wasn't enough they'd take your life.'

Chloris started talking about one of their neighbours. She said he was a 'greasy little wop' who drives around in a pickup truck trying to pick up women.

'Does he have GREASY LITTLE WOP painted on the side of the truck?' I asked. Joan nudged my knee with her foot.

'No', said Chloris. 'He doesn't have to. Anyone can see it's a greasy little wop behind the wheel.'

I figured she was just annoyed because he'd never tried to pick her up.

Chloris and Tinker Bell were telling Joan about the Ogre, Tinker Bell's husband, and how he used to be such a great guy but lately he's turned mean.

'He phones her up from work all the time and wants to know what she's doing, the bastard', said Chloris. 'He wants to make sure she's doing all the housework.'

Tinker Bell nodded. 'Yeah', she said, 'and if I'm not in he sometimes phones over here.'

'That's right', said Chloris. 'He often phones here during the day looking for her. I just tell him I don't know where she is even if she's standing right next to me.'

Don and I were listening from the living room. 'He used to be a wonderful guy, really', said Don. 'He's six-foot-four and she's only four-foot-nine. He throws her around quite a bit. She doesn't like to admit it but he does. Sometimes she comes over here black and blue and sobbing her eyes out.'

'God', I said.

'Yeah, we used to be the greatest of friends. He got along really well with little Tania. They used to play together. He was just like a big overgrown kid with her. Then one day they were fooling around and little Tania accidentally kneed him in the balls. He grabbed her like this ... and began shaking her. When she came home and told me that I was so mad. If he ever does it again I tell you I'll kill him. I know I will. I'll kill him.'

'Do they have any children?' I felt as if I should be puffing meditatively on a pipe.

'No. And that's another thing. He wants kids and she refuses to get pregnant. She won't have any kids by him. Can't say I blame her.'

'What does he do for a living?'

'He manages a McDonald's Hamburger place.'

Tinker Bell came into the living room. She looked uncertain and very timid.

'Come here', said Don. 'Sit down.'

'Your feet are in the way.'

He sat up and pulled her down at one end of the sofa. He

grabbed her arm and looked at it. Then he frowned. 'What are these marks?'

She became even more embarrassed. 'I don't know. I can't remember where I got those.'

'Okay then. Rub my feet.' Now I was getting embarrassed.

She took his bare feet in her hands and began massaging them expertly. I could hear all those tiny bones cracking. My own feet began twitching with jealousy. She kept it up. 'Ah, that feels good', he said. 'Why didn't you ever do that before?'

'I did', she said. 'Don't you remember New Year's Eve?'

'Oh yeah.'

She got embarrassed again. 'What's your wife going to say when she comes in and sees me massaging your feet?' I think Chloris was in the bathroom.

'She can't complain', said Don. 'She never massages them herself. They have to be massaged by someone.'

Suddenly in stormed Chloris. 'I heard that', she said. She looked really angry and she looked as if she would have expressed her anger a lot more strongly if Joan and I hadn't been in the house.

Tinker Bell got up and came over to sit beside me. She looked as if she wanted to massage my feet. I would have let her but I was a little too nervous. There seemed to be a lot of tension in the air. I know it sounds stupid, but I couldn't help feeling as if something awful were about to happen.

91
A Visit to Tinker Bell's Place

Joan and I finally got into the van at four-thirty in the morning and immediately dropped into sound sleep. Two hours later I was awakened by the alarm clock in my bladder. I slipped out of the van and tried to get into the house but all the doors were locked. That didn't seem right. When you have guests sleeping in a van in your driveway it's only common courtesy to leave a door open. But then I remembered this was the United States. All that suburban paranoia really prevailed. They were afraid of gangs of murdering Mau Maus bursting into their house in the middle of the night. I pissed in the rose bushes. I hoped the Ogre wasn't looking out his window.

When we finally got up Chloris made a glorious July 4 breakfast for all of us. Fried eggs, bacon, mushrooms, orange juice, toast, twelve kinds of jam. Yum. As I ate, Don handed me his stereo headphones. His beloved Pink Floyd record was playing. *The Dark Side of the Moon.* I thought of the dark side of Lake Erie. But the music was nice to eat breakfast by. I really liked it a lot. He was pleased.

Tinker Bell came over and had tea with us. Then she took us over to her house to show it off. The Ogre was at work of course. At McDonald's, July 4 is a particularly big day.

The house was filled with big heavy imitation antique furniture. The walls were covered with pieces of silver from the Ogre's collection. There were silver spoons from all of the states, silver plaques representing various episodes from American history, and so on. The atmosphere was simply electric with dull patriotism.

I picked up the Cleveland *Plain Dealer* and read a front-page exposé on some conniving congressman. The reporter had done an absolutely wonderful job. 'God, they've really nailed this guy', I said. 'He's finished.'

Don was less than enthusiastic. He disliked newspapers. 'Yeah, they nailed Sam Shepherd too', he said. 'They nailed him on circumstantial evidence. That paper gets away with murder.'

I spent the rest of the visit playing with the dogs. The collie was particularly susceptible to my caresses. I really know what dogs like.

On the wall was a wedding photo. It was a large head shot of the Ogre superimposed on a full-length photo of Tinker Bell in her wedding dress. Very artistic. Tinker Bell looked apprehensive, her head bowed towards her bridal bouquet. The Ogre looked like Robert Redford. Tinker Bell had aged a lot in two years.

92
A Stupid Computer in Buffalo

The heat was horrendous. I felt like an Eskimo lost in the Sahara. I don't know why we did this but we put Bruce in the van along with a fresh bowl of water and rolled the windows up with only about a three-inch clearance. 'There's a lot of dognappers around here', said Don. 'And that's no mutt you got there. They just love to get their hands on dogs like that.'

We thought we were only going to be gone for fifteen minutes but it was almost three hours before we returned. They took us to Uncle Bill's, the only department store open July 4. It was the 201st birthday of the United States of America and to celebrate I bought a skateboard for my daughters. Theirs had been stolen in Canada.

Then I saw this vinyl snap-on steering wheel cover for three dollars and I bought it like a fool. It was all sealed in a transparent plastic package. Later when I ripped it out of its casing and tried to put it on the steering wheel it turned out to be the tackiest thing I'd ever wasted my money on. I finally threw it in the garbage.

Joan found a bathing suit she really liked and I told her she'd probably find a nicer one in Canada. She put it back. What a rat! I'm worse than the Ogre in my own way. Months later she was still telling me she wished she'd ignored me and bought it. She says she's never seen one that suited her so well.

The record shop next door was open as well. They had Bob Marley's new record, *Exodus,* which I bought much to my later regret. After listening to it for five minutes I realized he'd finally cleaned up his Jamaican nationalist act and sold his soul to get on the US charts. Exodus indeed. The next one will be called *You Can't Go Home Again.*

I also bought a blank tape at Don's urging. 'You can tape my Pink Floyd record and listen to it whenever you want, he said. The strangest thing is this: I didn't feel guilty at the time about stopping Joan from buying that bathing suit.

But to get a tape at that store you reach your hand through a hole in the padlocked transparent plastic door just like in Canadian stores. But then you pull the tape you want towards you and let it fall onto a conveyor belt. I'd never seen that before. The conveyor belt takes it up to the cash register. 'What won't they think of next?' I said.

The clerk was standing there. She looked like a young Ursula Andress. 'You never know, she said.

She was calling out questions to the head clerk, a black guy.

'Are the Heptones soul or jazz?' she said.

'Reggae, I called out.

'No, it's soul, said the black guy, apologetically.

'What?' I said. 'Who decides that?'

'Oh, some stupid computer in Buffalo, he said, with passion.

'Kee-rist, I said. 'Do you play the tape for the computer and it decides what category the music falls into?'

'No, it's not that sophisticated, he said. 'The guy who programs the computer knows absolutely nothing about music.'

93

Race Relations in Painesville

We were back in Don's air-conditioned van. Don and I were up front, the women and kids in the back. 'That's where we first saw you, little Tania screamed out as we passed that critical point on the US 20. I didn't know where we were going and I was beginning to worry about Bruce. 'You waved at me, remember?'

'Oh yeah, I remember, I said. I always like to wave at kids we pass on the highway.

We were being taken on a tour of Don McFadden's general environment. We went through Painesville. Don told us it had been the locale for a famous movie about thirty years before but he couldn't remember the name of the movie. It was something about a white woman who falls in love with a black man. 'Back then this was the only town in the United States where a movie like that could be made', he said, without emotion.

'Why was that?'

'The race relations here were excellent.'

'That's strange with a name like Painesville.'

'Yeah, that is kinda funny.'

'And how are the race relations now?'

'Probably about the same.'

I told him about an incident that happened in North Carolina a while back. I went into a country store and there were four guys sitting around watching television. Two were white and two were black. The white guys were sitting on chairs. One of the black guys was sitting on the floor, the other kneeling on the floor. I was buying a six-pack. There was a little blob of blood on the counter where somebody had placed some fresh meat.

94
Race Relations in North Carolina

'I don't like the sight of that blood', said one of the white guys. He motioned to one of the black guys. 'Clean it up.'

'Yessir', the black guy said, scrambling. He ran back with a J-cloth. 'Where's the Windex gone?' he said. In a moment he was back with a bottle of Windex. He cleaned off the entire counter.

I was a little embarrassed. I was counting out my change to pay for the six-pack and I dropped a dime on the floor. Before I could bend down to pick it up, the same white guy turned to the other black guy and said, 'Pick that up for the man.'

The man yet. Imagine! The black guy went so fast he was just a blur. In a split second the dime was back in my hand and the black guy was back at his spot on the floor watching the boob tube. I had the feeling the white guy was showing off. He probably figured I was from the northern United States and he was demonstrating that the Civil War was all in vain. He still had his slaves. An extremely efficient form of technology. Wasn't I envious? It was quite macho, like gunning a hotrod at a stoplight.

We were staying at a motel right next to the country store. In the morning the good old boy who ran the motel wanted to talk so I decided to try to explore the situation a little in my own sneaky way.

'You know', I said, 'when I knew I was coming down here I was expecting to see a lot of bad feeling between the blacks and the whites. But I haven't seen anything like that anywhere. Why, **93** last night I went into that country store to get me some beer and I saw two white guys and two black guys sitting there watching television together just as if they were old friends. I'm really impressed.'

The good old boy started purring like a kitten. 'We've got some really sweet niggers down here,' he said. 'I think all the sour niggers went up north. Yes sir, I figure I've got as many nigger friends as white friends. Maybe even more. Of course that was a public place where you saw them watching television. We would never let them in our living rooms. We good friends but not on a social basis. If some niggers wanted to stay at this motel I'd put them right at the back. Of course there are certain white people I'd put right at the back too.'

The guy said he felt there was no north and south anymore. 'It's just one country as far as I'm concerned,' he said. He started talking about some awful disease that had been hitting his hunting dogs. Tears filled his eyes as he told of how they died in agony. Some of them he had to shoot.

95

A Feeling of Utter Death in the Air

A lot of blacks would have been better off down there than moving up here and spending their lives working in sweatshops, said Don. The guy's basically right. The blacks up here are really sour. That's why they're always killing each other. It's a big problem.

He also said blacks and whites don't even get together in public places in Ohio, never mind socially. 'That's good,' he said. 'The South is really progressing. We're not.'

We drove through a couple of shopping centres even though they were closed for the holiday. Chloris showed us the store where she used to work.

'What department did you work in?' said Joan.

'*Exclusive* sports wear,' said Chloris. 'Quite expensive.'

There were stores everywhere. It was like a fix. It was getting sickening. I wanted out of it all. I waxed philosophical. 'What a consumer society!' I said. 'All we do is work to buy and buy to work.'

No answer.

We passed a small factory. 'That's Towmotor, where I work,' said Don in a small voice. It looked like a shoebox with some chimneys.

'Nice place,' I said.

We passed the Holden Arboretum and the first Mormon Temple to be built in the United States (still in use). We cut up some back roads and passed a Girl Scout troop on a hike. There were hundreds of them.

We passed through a series of little towns dominated by service stations, shopping centres and McDonald's restaurants. Everytime we passed a McDonald's I'd say, 'Is that where the Ogre works?' It never was.

It was all getting rather dismal. There was a feeling of utter death in the air. No excitement. Just gloom gloom gloom. This is what Canada will be like some day, when there is nothing left to fight for, I thought. *Les Québécois* had the right idea. Independence wasn't the question, but the fight for independence was. Thank God there is still something left fighting for in my country, still something left to be created. Maybe I was fooling myself. Maybe things were worse than I thought.

96
Naked in a Foreign Country

We were back in North Skylark. We passed a shopping centre. It was about the ninety-seventh we'd passed that day. I noticed a large OPEN sign in front of a pizza store. 'Let's order a couple of pizzas,' I said.

So we stopped and I ran in and ordered two large pizzas: one with pepperoni and sausage the way the American McFaddens like it and one with double cheese and mushrooms the way the Canadian McFaddens like it. We didn't tell them about the horsemeat / pepperoni scandal that hit the Niagara Peninsula and Montreal a few years back. Goddamned Mafia!

'What's the name?' said the guy in the red apron and funny hat. He had a thin moustache like Clark Gable but was much fatter. Most Americans look like somebody famous.

'McFadden,' I said, feeling naked in a foreign country. Did he know I was a Canadian? I felt as if I weren't a real McFadden, just a counterfeit. The real McFadden was in the driver's seat in the van.

'It'll be ready in twenty minutes,' said Clark Gable.

97
Dogs Are Tough

Then I remembered Bruce. We decided to head back, check Bruce, drop off the women and kids, then drive back to the pizza store.

When we reached the McFaddens' place I hopped out of the van and into mine to rescue Bruce. He was gasping a little, all his water was gone, but he seemed all right.

We let Bruce lie down in the cool shade and rinsed him off with a cold rag. He seemed to enjoy all the attention. Dogs don't hold grudges. They're instantly forgiving. Then Don and I went back to pick up the pizza.

While we were gone, Joan later told me, they went around the back and found one of the McFaddens' dogs hanging from the fence. He had tried to climb over the fence and had been hanging there gasping all the time we were gone in all that heat. They released him and he appeared to be all right. That was Bobby, the one who could climb Mount Everest. Unfortunately he was never going to get the chance. Just like the untold geniuses who died in concentration camps.

98
Smoking Hashish in Ohio

As we drove around the corner Don pulled out his hash pipe and handed it to me. 'You feel like a little toke?' he said.

'Sure.' I lit up.

'Don't tell Chloris though. She can't stand the idea of me smoking. She'd go apeshit.'

'Yeah, women are really stupid.' Imagine a veteran of a major foreign war coming home and being told by his wife what he can and can't smoke. It just wasn't right. We McFaddens had to stick together.

I took one puff of the hash and my head melted away until I was cut off at the neck. I handed the pipe to Don. He took two puffs. 'Want more?' he said.

'Next year maybe,' I said.

99
A Brave American

The guy said the pizzas would be ready in another minute or two. Don and I waited outside. It was slightly cooler there than inside with all the ovens.

A red Chevy van pulled up. The girl behind the wheel was an incredible sight for someone a little high on cannabis. She was wearing a neck collar, a head bandage, a chin bandage, and she had two black eyes. Her eyes were little swollen slits. Her jaws were wired shut.

She looked at us. 'Is this store open?' she said.

'Yes, it is,' I managed to get out.

She got out of the van. We couldn't help gawking at her. She was covered in bruises and cuts. Bandages were falling off her. She had one arm in a cast, the other in a sling. She pulled her crutches out of the van.

ERIE

'Holy Christ!' I muttered. In my state I felt as if she had endured the most incredible atrocities ever devised.

'I bet she was in a motorcycle spill,' said Don.

She started swinging her body in the direction of the stereo store. It was closed. I thought she'd meant the pizza store. How could I have been so stupid?'

'Oh, I'm so sorry,' I said. 'I thought you meant the pizza store.'

The girl shrugged and swung her body back to the van.

'What happened to you?' said Don.

'Motorcycle spill,' she said.

'I thought so,' said Don. 'Gonna keep ridin'?'

'You bet. Soon's I get these casts off.'

'Good for you.'

Our feet weren't quite touching the ground as we floated into the McFadden back yard with the pizzas. We placed them on a little card table that had miraculously appeared.

'Isn't that wonderful?' I said. 'A card table to put the pizza on!'

'Yeah,' said Don. 'What won't they think of next?'

Strangely enough, Chloris and Joan didn't seem to think anything amiss. Everyone grabbed a piece of pizza, except Chloris. 'I'm on a diet,' she said, sternly.

'A diet? You? A skinny little thing like you?' I said.

'Yes, a diet,' she said, without a trace of amusement. She knew she wasn't skinny, although she wasn't as fat as the average Georgia sheriff.

'Well, you've got pretty good willpower,' I said. 'This pizza is almost as good as they make in Hamilton.'

'I don't like Italian food,' she said.

'She doesn't like Italians period,' said Don.

'Oh yeah, I forgot. Well,' I said, 'you could have said something before we got it.' I went on and on. 'We could have got something else. We could have gone to a restaurant and all had something different. You could have had a little chef's salad with no-cal dressing ...'

'No,' she said, sharply. 'It's all right.' She sounded a little weary, as if she were ready for us to go. Well, we weren't quite ready yet. We'd go when we bloody well felt like it. After all, we hadn't invited ourselves.

Even Don was getting a little tired. He had to go to work that night and his body was telling him to prepare for it by having a sleep.

The kids all wanted to go in for one last swim.

'You sure you don't mind, Chloris?' said Joan.

'No,' she said, wearily. 'Let them go in if they must.'

So they went in. Chloris's impatience was colouring the whole atmosphere.

'Where's that blank tape?' said Don. 'I might as well tape *The Dark Side of the Moon* for you.'

'Oh yeah.' We went in the house. I put on the headphones and listened as he taped. The music sounded absolutely sensational. I floated away on a pillowy cloud of nothingness to the very place we would have been if I hadn't bothered waving at little Tania McFadden on the road. Somewhere beyond the horizon where the planets exert different influences on earthly life and time goes sideways, back and forth. To paraphrase Roy Kiyooka: Thank you, everyone, for helping me dream this dream.

Mentioning other writers in your writing is 'a fault of youth and inexperience,' wrote the Toronto poet and science fiction writer Phyllis Gotlieb in the winter 1978 issue of *Quarry*. Please, God, let me never become old and experienced.

Thank you, Roy Kiyooka, for helping me dream this dream in which we are drawing a circle of light around Lake Erie.

A dream in which everything within that circle is ours.

101

Consciousness

Chloris was telling us all about the various races she didn't like and why she didn't like them. Italians were the most disliked. Joan told her she should never come to visit us because we were the only non-Italians on the street.

Chloris also hated the Spanish, the Greeks, the Germans and the Irish. She didn't mention Jews, Arabs, Africans or Orientals. I think it went without saying that all four were on her hate list.

Everyone was sitting around in the living room. They were ignoring me totally. I had the headphones on and was pretending to be absorbed in the music. They didn't realize the right headphone wasn't covering my ear and I could hear every word that was being spoken.

But I didn't realize the kids were paying attention too. Then innocent little Alison piped up. 'We have some Irish blood in us,' she said. She was obviously wondering if that meant we were no good.

Chloris' brain snapped like a steel trap. 'I didn't know Irish had blood,' she said. Alison frowned.

I felt sick. I thought of that horrendous line from Camoens.

Vasco da Gama has just greeted a flotilla of Moslems from Mozambique and says: 'We come from Europe, the home of strong and warlike peoples'.

Chloris spoke again about the possibility of moving to New Zealand. She thought she'd really like the country because the people there were all English or Scotch and had little tolerance for people of other racial origins. I thought that was eminently sensible and realistic of her.

'Maybe New Zealand will turn out to be your spiritual home', said Joan, sympathetic as always.

'I think you might be right', said Chloris.

'I could live anywhere, I could', said Don, sweetly.

'Dave's four grandparents were Irish, Scotch, Welsh and English', said Joan. 'So he's a real mongrel'.

Everyone looked over at me. My eyes were unfocussed and I seemed to be drifting along with the music. I gave no indication I was following the discussion.

'He's British', said Chloris. I don't know whether she decided that on my looks, my name, or what Joan had just told her.

'Don't you hold it against him that he's part Irish?' said Joan.

'Not really. He can't help being part Irish. He doesn't act Irish. That's the main thing'.

That got me thinking. I sort of felt Irish. Sometimes in fact I feel like a pure southern Irishman in exile, exile from the one true church and one true homeland. And I think I look Irish. I think James Joyce had a friend who looked just like me. I like to dress up in clothes I imagine would be in style in Dublin in 1920. In *Ulysses* there's a minor character named Babyface McFadden the Cop. When I finished reading Joyce's letters I cried. I don't know why.

But mostly I hate being European. Europeans are the dregs of the human race as far as I'm concerned. They're so ugly too, compared to Orientals, Africans, American Indians. We're beginning to learn our lesson but it's too late. We're really almost extinct according to demographers. Take the Germans for instance. There won't be any Germans in Europe by 2050 according to a recent demographic study. Sort of ironic, isn't it?

And although there are a lot of McFaddens in Scotland, McFadden is definitely an Irish name. I guess Don never told Chloris that. He was probably afraid to. Like he was afraid to smoke grass at home. Little did she know she was married to a member of the very race she most despised. Lovely. Her own children were half-Irish. Yuk yuk.

But none of us can help what we are. A little philosophy here. **99**

The personality is the mask. The only thing in control is the unadulterated indivisible consciousness we all share. The stuff that fills the universe like radio waves, the stuff we as biological creatures, as genetic robots, merely receive like radios, like fine tuning mechanisms.

102
The Dark Side
of the Moon

There seemed to be some amazing energy transfers going on between Chloris and Donald.

Both were strong, independent personalities. Yet sometimes when Don was talking you could see his personality dissolve and Chloris' take over. Other times when Chloris was talking, Don's personality would take over. Almost in a hypnotic way.

For instance, Don likes Pink Floyd and motorcycles and is decidedly anti-American – at least until someone else starts attacking his country. Yet he found my Bob Marley tapes from Jamaica too nationalistic for his liking. I wish I'd had my Stompin' Tom Connors tapes along. And when he began talking about the Punk Rock fad that was at its height that summer he expressed deep concern that it would have a harmful influence on his children. When he said that his own personality seemed to conk out and Chloris's took over.

Further, Chloris hates Pink Floyd and any kind of rock and roll. She would complain whenever Don played his records. She particularly hated Don's favourite record, *The Dark Side of the Moon.*

But at one point I was sitting in the living room with Chloris and decided to compliment her on her furniture.

'It's quite elegant in a regal sort of way', I said. 'One glance at it and I could tell you are a monarchist, if you'll forgive me for psychoanalyzing you through your interior decor.'

'Royal blue would be more appropriate for the British monarchy', she said. 'This red would suit the Spanish monarchy perhaps.'

Then she began talking about Pink Floyd. She began telling me how *The Dark Side of the Moon* represents death and rebirth. She became quite excited about it and used almost the same words Don had used earlier in explaining the hidden symbolism of the music. Again, she in turn seemed to have conked out and Don's personality seemed to be shining through.

'I thought you didn't like that record', I said. I was astounded when her own personality came back like the crack of a whip.

'I *don't* like it', she snarled. 'I hate it. But I listened to it carefully and that's just the impression I got.'

We were finally leaving. The kids looked sad. Chloris looked relieved. Don looked tired. Tinker Bell came over to say good-bye and she looked apprehensive.

I took several photos. I got a shot of Don holding a hangman's noose over Joan's head. I tried to get everyone in a lineup from shortest to tallest but there was no co-operation. For one thing Chloris wouldn't allow me to take her picture.

I kept trying to deke her out, trying to snap a picture so fast she wouldn't notice. But she was too wary for me. I got a couple of good shots of the back of her head. I got a picture of her behind a tree. But no picture of her face. That's all right. I've got a lot of pictures of Margaret Laurence who looks just like her.

When we were pulling out I said I was going to write to the Ohio department of tourism and suggest they give a gold medal to the McFadden Family of North Skylark. 'For by your generosity and fine spirit of brotherhood, your warmth and hospitality and your high regard for the principles of freedom and democracy, you have made a significant gesture that in the long run can serve only to increase the ties between Ontario and Ohio ...' I went on and on.

'That's because we're not Americans', said Chloris with a snarl. 'Americans wouldn't have done this'.

We drove down to Skylark-on-the-Lake then east along the Lake Erie shore. We were quiet, looking peacefully out at the lake, wondering about the tiny grey rectangles steaming along out at the horizon.

'You know the way Chloris didn't want her picture taken?' I said.

'Yes?' said Joan.

'Do you think I was stupid for trying to sneak a picture of her like that? I was just doing it to try to make her feel better. Do you think I should have let it drop?'

'Yeah, I think you should have'.

As we approached Ashtabula the lakefront became more indus-trialized, with smokestacks and docks all over the place. You know, even now, months later, I still haven't got those damned pictures developed. I should apply to the Canada Council for money to get all my pictures from the past five years developed.

All of a sudden we noticed a young man walking along with a baby in his arms. 'Look at that poor young fellow', I said. 'He seems way too young to be burdened with a baby.'

We were driving slow. Joan looked. 'Where?' she said. I pulled over quietly.

'Over there.'

'I see the guy but where's the baby?'

I looked again. Sure enough there was no baby in his arms. Had I been seeing things? The fellow was walking nervously away from the dock and towards an old bashed-in Chrysler. As he opened the door to get in someone ran up to him and grabbed him from behind. I couldn't believe it.

The guy shot his elbow back and caught his attacker in the teeth. Then several other guys – they looked like dockworkers – ran up. The guy got into his car in a hurry and was trying to drive away and lock the doors from the inside at the same time but the dockworkers managed to get the door open and pull him out. There were about four of them. They pulled him to the ground and sat on him.

We had an excellent view of the action. When we first looked it was quite a lonely scene. Just a fellow walking at dockside with a baby in his arms. Now there was no baby but the scene was filled with hysterical people running all over the place. A Coast Guard patrol boat pulled up at the dock and someone dove into the water. A moment later someone was climbing to the deck of the patrol boat with a baby in his arms.

So now it was clear. The guy must have thrown his baby into the water and had been trying to get away. A lot of people like us must have been watching him from a distance. Some must have been watching more carefully than we were.

We could see the baby in the boat. They were covering it with blankets. It was obviously alive.

A police cruiser pulled up and then three more. They released the guy from the dockworkers' hold. He seemed to be offering no resistance. All the cops had their guns drawn. There were about twenty guns pointing at this poor unarmed kid. One cop stepped up and pulled the kid's head back while another cop handcuffed him.

We decided to move on. By this time there were dozens of cars stopped at the side of the road, gawking, like us. We couldn't have been any assistance. We hadn't seen the kid throw the baby or drop it or whatever. Others obviously had. So any evidence we could have given at his trial would have been worthless.

Strange thinking about the incident now. Where is the guy at this moment? Where is the baby?

We pulled into a campground just over the Pennsylvania state line. It was called Shangri-La Holiday Park. Smiling happy faces. Who could resist it?

We bought some milk and bread in the camp store and asked the price of a campsite.

'Four twenty-five,' said the woman behind the counter. She looked like Dolly Parton.

'What? That's outrageous,' I said jokingly.

'Well, if you don't like it,' she said, pausing slightly, 'you can go down the road apiece. They're a lot cheaper. But if you want hot-and-cold showers, a pool table, and lots of recreational facilities including canoes, and nice clean campsites, and a lot of other features too numerous to mention, you'll just have to pay four twenty-five at least.'

She didn't mention the showers and pool table were coin-operated, and you had to pay extra for the canoes.

'Where y'all from?' she said.

'Hamilton,' I said, assuming she'd think I meant Hamilton, Ohio.

'Oh, we've been there,' she said. 'On the way up to Tobermory, right?'

I smiled. 'Right.'

'We went over this big bridge and you could just barely see Hamilton through the smog. Smoky city. Whatch y'all doin' down here?'

'We just came down to get a breath of fresh air, eh?'

'Oh!' She thought for a moment. 'Hey, you got lots of fresh air up there. Don't try'n fool me. I been up there lotsa times. I jest love Canadians. They're so much fun. I love to hear them say ... "eh?" I start doin' it myself after awhile. Eh?'

I couldn't figure out what Canadians she'd met who were so much fun. Must have been some *French*-Canadians, eh?

I gave her the four twenty-five. She handed me a green garbage bag and said, 'That's for your garbage.'

'You mean you want us to put our *garbage* in there?'

'That's right,' she said, smiling. She was beginning to think maybe I'd be a lot of fun too if she only gave me half a chance.

'But we just like to throw our garbage around on the ground. And in the woods and all that. We don't like being neat on our holidays.'

'Oh, you're jest foolin.' You Canadians are pretty neat people. You never see any garbage on the ground in Canada. You see green garbage bags jest full to burstin' and neatly tied. You see them everywhere you go in Canada.'

She handed me a wooden coin and said, 'Now that's a wooden nickel. You just hang on to that and the next time you're down this way you come here and you get a fifty-cent reduction.'

I looked at the coin. It had a picture of an Indian chief on it. He had a big goofy smile on his face. But all his feathers were in place. It looked as if it had been drawn by one of those guys who draw for *Mad*.

106
The Black Lung

We found a nice campsite under a little grove of maple trees. The campgrounds had been carved out of what looked like a virgin forest featuring huge elms and oaks among the pine, cedar and spruce. Night was falling.

There was some firewood on our campsite so I started a roaring campfire – again with one match.

The four of us were sitting there watching the flames.

'I know a girl who has hair the colour of those flames,' said Alison, poetically.

'What's her name?' I said.

'Rachel.'

'I know a girl who has hair the colour of that sky,' said Jennifer. The sky was dark, no moon.

'What's *her* name?' I said.

'Hughdel,' said Jennifer.

'I know two little girls who are really tired,' said Joan, 'and should be put to bed right away.'

'What's their names?' said Jennifer.

'Alison and Jennifer,' said Joan.

Then along came Morley, the guy who ran the place. He was riding a white bicycle. He had a black beard and a high-pitched voice. He and his bicycle were illuminated by the flames.

'I just came to see if y'all got settled in all right. And you sure are. You've even found some firewood left behind by another camper and got a fire going.' He'd been cheated out of a dollar for firewood. That's what they charged. He was a little overweight.

'You're going to lose weight if you ride on your bicycle to every campsite every night,' said Joan.

'I hope so,' said Morley, proudly patting his belly.

He told us he came from a town called Grand Rapids, Minnesota, which was a few miles northwest of Duluth. He said he was just passing through Erie, Pennsylvania, one day, met a girl and never left. That was the girl we met on the way in, the one who looked like Dolly Parton.

'You never know when it's going to happen,' he told us. We

nodded sagely. He said the two of them liked to go skin-diving in Tobermory every summer. 'I just love Canadians', he said.

He pointed to a trailer a little down the lane. He said it belonged to a retired coal miner with the Black Lung. He said the miner lives in the trailer all year long.

'In the winter he takes his trailer to Florida and in the summer he brings it back up here to Pennsylvania'.

Morley told us he didn't run the campground full time. 'I have to do other work', he said. 'But I hope maybe in about ten years I'll be able to do this full time'.

We asked him about his other job.

'I'm an electrician in construction', he said.

There were a lot of women with bee-hive hairdos, little dogs that barked too much, and a lot of fat, hairy-shouldered men in baggy undershirts and knee-length baggy shorts. You could see them walking up and down the lane, with flashlights. Flames from campfires and electric lights from campers and big Winnebagos illuminated their features.

107
Black Motorcycle Gangs

Morley was still leaning against his white bicycle. We told him a little about our trip, including our trip through Cleveland. We told him how surprised we were by the city, and impressed.

'The coloured pretty well own that town', he said.

Then he began telling us a long, involved, and seemingly pointless story about two black kids from Buffalo whose motorcycle had a flat on the US 5 in front of the Shangri-La Holiday Park one day.

'They came in and asked us if they could use the phone. I said sure. So they phoned a friend in Buffalo and asked him to bring his van down here and fix their tire. I told them they could just take it a mile up the road to old Smitty's and he'd fix it for them. But they thought I was just tryin' to get rid of them'.

'So what happened?'

'I don't know. But the van never did make it. It broke down half way'.

I neglected to ask him how they finally got their flat fixed.

'Yeah', I said. 'I notice quite a few black people on motorcycles. In fact we saw some black motorcycle gangs. You ever get them coming in here?' The idea tickled me.

Morley looked a little worried, as if such talk could make something that horrible come true. 'No', he said. 'We don't let any motorcyclists in here, white or black. If they complain we just call the state troopers. They can complain to them'.

'But you never see any black people in campgrounds in the States,' I said. 'Why would that be, Morley?'

He looked a little nervous again. 'I had a black family in here just the other day,' he said. 'No problem at all.'

I could hardly hear Morley any more because someone had jacked up the volume on a radio across the lane. About twenty people from different campsites were crowded around drinking beer and listening to a ball game. They must have been deaf. Or they soon would be.

108
The Prince
of Peace

Just after Joan and I jumped into bed and shut the door of the van rain started to hit the roof. Then it really started coming down. I peeked out my window and watched the campfire go down to defeat in the elemental battle.

It rained all night. About six-thirty I was awakened by a guy gunning his motor about twenty feet away. I couldn't believe it. I was amazed that Joan and the kids could sleep through it. He kept on and on. I was waiting for him to stop so I could go back to sleep but it looked as if he were going to keep gunning that engine for all eternity.

He wasn't stuck in the mud or anything like that. He was just gunning his motor. I pushed aside the curtain and glared at him. He couldn't see me. He was just sitting there in the driver's seat gunning his motor. He must have been in some kind of trance.

So I put on my jeans and went outside in the rain. I told him to keep it down, I was trying to sleep.

He was a thin fellow, wiry, about sixty years old. He didn't say anything. He just got out of his car, slammed the door as hard as he could and went into his trailer.

I noticed he had Georgia licence plates. On the back of his trailer was a sign saying THE PRINCE OF PEACE.

109
Porky the
Coal Miner

I stayed outside waiting for Joan and the kids to begin to stir. If I went back into the van to try to catch another hour's sleep I would have wakened them. So I just sat there. The rain stopped. But the maple trees were full of rainwater and every time there was a gust of wind the water came down as if it were still raining.

I kept hoping to catch a glimpse of the coal miner with the Black Lung. He sounded like a really romantic figure. Someone to write about.

Finally I saw him. He came out of his trailer and started swatting flies. Nothing like a little massacre to start the day. He was entirely unlike my expectations. He was short and fat, wore shorts, a baggy undershirt and a funny hat, and had a high-pitched drawl. His wife called him Porky. She was still in the trailer as he continued swatting flies outside and calling out the score.

'Thirty-seven, dear', he called out. Then, after a few seconds, 'Thirty-nine, got two that time!'

Finally the sun came over the trees and started to dry things out and shed some warmth. Porky's high-pitched squeal continued.

'The haymaker's comin' out', he squeaked.

I couldn't figure out what he meant at first. Then he said, 'The sun's startin' to shine.' I guess the haymaker is an affectionate term for the sun. The term had probably been in his family for generations.

Some coal miner! His trailer was called 'The Aristocrat.'

'Hope you get over the Black Lung', I whispered, insincerely.

As I sat under the wet trees waiting for Joan and the kids to wake up I really felt as if we were camped among the enemy. I couldn't help it. We were camped among a powerful, complacent race of people who could eliminate other races or cultures at a whim. 'We can destroy the entire world if we want', they seemed to be whispering.

The people who had been listening to the baseball game the night before weren't stirring. I went for a walk.

A huge fat man in jeans got out of a small tent trailer with 'Little Injun' painted on the side. He might have called it 'Little Nigger' but knew better.

At another campsite just down the lane a plastic sign was nailed to a tree. On the sign was a picture of a trailer and a coffee pot with a steaming happy face. You can buy these signs in camping stores I guess and they come complete with blank spaces in which you are intended to have printed your name and home state. This sign read: 'Hi There Welcome Neighbors. Darn Good Coffee. We Are The MARTIN's From The Great State Of ERIE, PA.'

110
The Great State of Erie, Pa.

I walked past a weedy, scum-covered pond about the size of a septic tank. Three freshly painted canoes were pulled up on the grassy shore. They were numbered: 1, 2, 3. Sitting there, they looked just like the number 111 which happens to be the number of this chapter. What a coincidence! A little stream trickled out of

111
Canoes for Rent

the woods and into the pond. Just beyond the pond (beyond the pond?) was a building housing the camp store, headquarters and recreation centre.

Morley's wife was behind the counter again. She looked even more like Dolly Parton this morning with her oversized breasts sticking straight out like nose cones and her long hair piled up into a hay stack on top of her head.

'Hello again,' I said.

'I usually don't see any campers stirring this early,' she said. 'Have a good night's sleep?'

I thought about the Prince of Peace. 'Don't ask,' I said.

'All right, I won't.'

She was a little wary of me, and was waiting to find out what I wanted so early in the morning.

'How much are your canoes?'

'Seventy-five cents an hour.'

'And where do you paddle them?'

I guess that was a stupid question. 'Why, in the pond of course,' she said, laughing.

'But the pond isn't much *bigger* than a canoe,' I said.

A cloud passed over her face. 'Why, *we* have a lot of fun with those canoes,' she said.

112

Shooting Pool with a Mass Murderer

So I strolled into the recreation hall and Dolly followed me. There was a thin, elderly black woman sweeping the floor. There was a coin-operated pool table, some pinball machines, and a lending library. The lending library was pretty sad: old movie magazines, cowboy novels from the fifties, a battered old copy of David McFadden's *A Trip around Lake Erie*.

I put a quarter in the pool table and the balls fell out of their little cage and spilled onto the felt. Dolly came scurrying over, noticing that Number 10 had failed to drop. She wanted to give me another quarter.

'No, it's all right. Honest. I'm just going to sink a few.'

Then all of a sudden this little girl appeared. I hadn't noticed her before. She had freckles, a cute little dress, pigtails, cute little patent-leather shoes, the whole bit. And she also had the most evil-looking face I'd ever seen. It was chilling. I couldn't figure out what it was about her face that signalled such evil so strongly.

'I'll play with you,' she said, grabbing a cue from the rack on the wall. 'Let me break them.' She pushed me. 'No, you break them. I want to see how good you are.'

108   'I'm no good,' I said. 'No good at all. I haven't played for years.'

'I'll break them then. I always like to break them.'

The old black cleaning lady stopped sweeping and looked over. She was smiling.

'You watch out for him, Michelle,' she said. 'All the sharks say they no good and haven't played fo' years.'

So Michelle broke the balls and I went to take a shot.

'No,' she screamed. 'It's still my shot. I sunk one.'

'See what ah tell ya,' said the old woman.

This went on and on. I couldn't believe it. The little girl was so bossy and evil-looking I was absolutely certain, as if I'd seen it in a crystal ball, that she was going to grow up to be a mass murderer. Maybe she was already. Maybe I was about to be her next victim.

I managed to make a graceful exit and scurried back to our campsite, feeling as if I were being stared at from behind the curtains of every Winnebago I passed.

No one was stirring in our van and so I sat down again under the trees. I was cold and miserable. The sun seemed to be going out.

Finally I couldn't stand it any longer so I whipped open the door to the van and woke up Joan and the kids.

'Let's just put the top down and pull out,' I said. 'We'll have breakfast in a restaurant on the road. You deserve a break today. I can't stand this place.'

Joan was immediately suspicious.

'Have you been in a fight or something?'

'No, no. It's just all muddy and every time there's a gust of wind the leaves drop cold water down your neck.'

Joan looked at me strangely. I realized I didn't sound very convincing. So I told her about the Prince of Peace and she was sure I'd had a fight with him.

'No I didn't. Honest.'

So we simply put the top down and drove away. Never to return.

We were driving east on Highway 5 looking for a likely spot to eat breakfast. Highway 5 wasn't marked on our Boron road map, but we figured out from conversations back at Shangri-La that it ran along the Lake Erie shore all the way to Buffalo.

'Do you see any difference between Pennsylvania and Ohio so far?' I asked Joan.

'Yeah,' said Joan without hesitation.

I could see it too. The road was a little snakier and not so flat. There were more vineyards and fewer commercial establishments. You could see the hills in the distance, dotted with prosperous old farms.

But I decided to play a trick on Joan. 'What?' I said. 'You can see a difference between Ohio and Pennsylvania already?' It was a cruel trick. Joan hates to appear stupid.

'No, I was just fooling,' she said.

'Oh, really? I can see a *big* difference,' I said.

'So can I,' said Joan.

'Let's stop at a Howard Johnson's for breakfast,' I said. 'We've never been in one of those yet.'

The first Howard Johnson's we came to was at the intersection of the US 5 and the road that runs into Presque Isle State Park on the outskirts of Erie, Pa. We pulled into the parking lot. Down the street was a McDonald's.

'Let's go to the McDonald's,' said Joan. 'They have nice breakfasts there. We've never been to a McDonald's yet, not for breakfast.'

I could read her mind. She thought the Howard Johnson's looked a little too spiffy for us, dressed as we were in dirty old camping clothes. And we hadn't even showered!

'We can go to McDonald's any old time,' I said. There was one right around the corner from us at home. (But our first visit to McDonald's for breakfast is documented in *A Trip around Lake Huron*.) 'Come on to the Howard Johnson's.'

'No!'

'Yes!'

'Oh, all right. Geez!'

115
Chocolate Milk

The Howard Johnson's was painted in red, white and blue. There were American eagle designs plastered all over it. You could tell the management believed wholeheartedly in the American way of life. Oh well, seeing is believing.

Joan was sitting in the car brushing her hair and looking at her face in the rearview mirror. Then she brushed the kids' hair. As soon as we went into the restaurant we headed straight for the washrooms to wash up a bit.

But you guessed it. When we finally got seated at our table we cautiously looked around and we were by far the best-dressed people in the place.

Sitting at the table across from us was a beautiful woman with beautiful long blond hair. But she was enormously fat from the neck down and was dressed in a food-stained blouse and thread-bare shorts, bursting at the seams. She was drinking chocolate milk. She looked like an overweight Jean Harlow.

I whispered to Joan: 'Check out this fat woman drinking chocolate milk for breakfast.'

Well that was it. The woman heard me. She glared at me then tossed her head just like in a 1940s Hollywood movie. I felt rotten.

The woman's daughter who was about five was also fat. She was drinking Coca-Cola.

'She heard you, you know,' said Joan, after a suitable pause.

'I know, I know,' I said. 'I can't do anything about it now. Unless you want me to go over and apologize to her.'

'I think you should,' said Joan.

'Okay, I will.' Joan was so sympathetic. I went to get up.

'Wait a minute,' said Joan. 'What are you going to say?'

'I don't know. I'll make it up as I go along.'

But when I got over to her table I couldn't think of anything to say.

'Excuse me, madame,' I said, standing there. 'I'd just like to apologize for my bad manners.' She and her daughter just stared ahead at their plates. They wouldn't even look at me. I felt truly ashamed. The atmosphere was very tense.

'Sometimes we say things we don't mean,' I said, 'and our voices carry further than we thought they would. I certainly didn't intend you to hear that. I'm not a cruel person.'

They still refused to acknowledge my presence so I shrugged and returned to my seat.

When the waitress, who looked like Audrey Hepburn, came to take our order she brought a huge steaming pot of coffee and placed it on the table. There must have been enough for twelve cups.

116
The S.S. North American

But when she took our orders and found out I wanted decaffein-ated coffee, Joan wanted tea and the kids wanted milk, she took it away.

She brought Joan one small pot of tea and me one small pot of Sanka. It didn't seem fair.

After we'd finished eating our eggs and pancakes and all that stuff, Joan went to the washroom again. The kids and I started playing catch with my ring of keys. We started giggling and hav-ing a great time. The keys went flying across the dining room several times and we had to take our turns bringing them back.

But when Joan came back we quietened down. Joan likes to be

sedate in restaurants. She likes to be serious like everyone else.

The dining room was panelled in mahogany, very well put together. I was admiring the carpentry.

'I like it but I think it's too dark for our place,' said Joan. We had been remodelling lately with money Joan earned as a supply teacher. The teacher she was filling in for had had a nervous breakdown so Joan got a solid two months in. Russell Seaworthy was doing a lot of the carpentry work.

Set in the wall next to our table was an illuminated glass case containing some old marine bells and a model of the S.S. *North American*. A beautiful model, really well done.

The card said the original was 310 feet long and was launched in 1913. It served as an excursion ship on the Great Lakes until the early sixties. It was lost in 'the mouth of the St. Lawrence' while being towed to the Caribbean in 1972.

'I wonder if anyone was drowned,' said Joan.

'I don't know,' I said. 'The first rule in writing is not to leave any unanswered questions — unless of course you're a poet.'

'Maybe the person who wrote this is a poet.'

'Maybe.'

117

A Monument to a Brave Commander

When we left Howard Johnson's we saw two teenage girls with towels under their arms. They were heading for the beach, trying to flag down rides.

'Should we pick them up?'

'No,' said Joan. 'The van's too messy. Just pull up beside them and I'll ask them the best way to get to the beach.'

So I pulled over and the girls told Joan the proper directions and all. And then Joan said, 'Could we give you a lift?'

The girls jumped in and I drove away, wonderingly. They said there were quite a few beaches to choose from, about nine in all. We dropped them off at Number 1. It was only about a mile from the restaurant.

Presque Isle State Park is a really beautiful series of lagoons, roads and beaches threading through a forest of poplars a hundred feet tall. You can see the city of Erie across the bay on the south side and Lake Erie on the north. We drove right to the end where there was a 150-foot monument 'erected by the State of Pennsylvania to commemorate the victory of Commodore Oliver Hazard Perry in the Battle of Lake Erie, Sept. 10, 1813.'

I thought of a nice little plaque to put under that one: 'We remember our victories, forget our defeats and begin to think we're invincible.'

It seemed strange to put such an impressive statue on the end of a sandbar just inches above the waters of a huge lake. The way the level of the Great Lakes is rising annually you'll soon have to paddle out to read the inscription.

By the way, Perry was the guy who, after destroying the British squadron on Lake Erie, said: 'We have met the enemy and they are ours,' which was altered by the late American cartoonist Walt Kelly, during the famous McCarthy hearings, to read: 'We have met the enemy and they are *us*' – which could mean different things to different people.

---

118 Junk Food

The fat people were out in force. Hundreds of them. In Canada everyone tries to keep as slim as possible. In the USA everyone tries to get as fat as possible. That's the big difference between the two countries.

All over Presque Isle State Park we saw these enormous men strutting around with their shoulders thrown back and their mammoth bellies sticking out like the prows of battleships. They all wore undershirts, shorts, hard black shoes and black *executive length* socks. They carried Polaroid cameras that fold up like notebooks, and they have police-like auras about them. They appear to be on the lookout for unamerican activities. They obviously know nothing about nutrition or if they do they choose to ignore what they know because life is so boring the only enjoyment they get is eating reams and reams of junk food. They don't want to go out at night for fear of getting mugged so they sit home watching TV and mugging the refrigerator.

'Goddamnit, Maw, there's no more junk food in the fridge.'

'Well listen, dear, why don't we just send out for some? What kinda junk food you wantin'?'

'I don't care as long as it's junk food. I'm just gonna die if I don't get some junk food inside me right quick.'

---

119 The Day Jennifer Almost Drowned

Presque Isle State Park is a thin brush stroke over the bare canvas of Lake Erie. We walked slowly in the heat through the poplars and onto the beach. We spread a blanket and sat down. There were signs all over saying keep your dog leashed. I hooked the loop on the end of Bruce's leash over my big toe. The kids went running into the grey water. A huge passenger jet on its way to New York City briefly blotted out the sun.

There was a lifeguard every 200 feet sitting high on a wooden platform like in an American movie starring Frankie Avalon and

Annette Funicello. We sat halfway between two of them. There were no dead fish on the beach. You could lie on the beach without coming up covered with grease.

'This beach is even better than the ones in Prince Edward Island', said Joan. 'And no jellyfish.'

It was the prevailing winds, I was convinced. They push all the crap over to the Canadian side. The prevailing winds come from the southwest and that's why during the summer it's always hot on the US side and cold on the Canadian side. The winds pick up moisture and coolness crossing the lakes. And the oil streaks, dead fish, dead gulls and raw sewage gets heaped up on the Canadian side.

But the important thing was to keep my eyes on the kids as they played in the water. Their heads were bobbing in the small waves. Some other kids had joined them. I counted six. So I just had to make sure there were always six out there. The lifeguards seemed more interested in their tans.

I had a copy of Robert Graves' short stories with me so I started reading 'A Toast to Ava Gardner' aloud to Joan. Every few lines I'd pause to make sure I could see six little heads bobbing out there.

But we soon became engrossed in the story.

And then I was up to the point where Ava and Robert begin discussing poetry, and Robert says: 'Poems are like people ... There are not many authentic ones around', when Joan interrupted me. I still can't get over how calmly she spoke.

'Dave', she said. 'Something's wrong. I can't see Jennifer.'

I stood up, still holding the book. I could see Alison, her head bobbing up and down in the little waves. She was out way too far. But I couldn't see Jennifer. My heart started sinking. Then I saw a little head come to the surface about fifteen feet further out than Alison's. It was Jennifer. Then I dropped the book, ripped off my watch and kicked off my sandals as I ran to the shoreline and kept running into the water. I was wearing cords and as soon as they hit the water they became lead casts. I didn't know whether running or swimming would be faster, nor did I know whether to pause long enough to take off my trousers. So I just kept running out until the water came up to my chest then started swimming furiously. I kept my eyes on where Jennifer's head had come to the surface then disappeared again.

When I got close to the spot her head came up again. Thank Christ! What luck! She was crying! 'Daddy', she said. I put my arms around her. I knew she was safe. If she had drowned I would have killed myself. 'I got out too far, Daddy', she said.

When we got back to shallow water a lot of people were standing at the shore tensely watching. I looked at one of the lifeguard platforms, and then the other. Incredibly, both lifeguards were just sitting there, not even looking in our direction, just peering straight out at the lake. That's all I saw before I collapsed right there on the sand, my toes still dangling in the water. Jennifer just slipped out of my arms, walked over to the blanket, picked up her copy of *Mad* and started reading.

A girl about eighteen came over after I resumed normal consciousness. She said that if I had been a few seconds later getting to Jennifer, she herself would have saved her. She had seen Jennifer going down and was racing in from another direction. That made me feel a lot better, really. 'God bless you,' I said, sort of emotionally. 'Are you a good swimmer?' She looked like she'd be a good swimmer and there were quite a few badges on her swim suit.

'I'm on the United States Olympic swimming team,' she said.

'Yeah?' I said, and I started crying.

The girl put her arm around me and suggested I go over to the blanket and sit down. I did. Then Joan put her arm around me too.

It turned out the girl was from Madison, Wisconsin, and was visiting some relatives in Erie. She really was on the Olympic team but I forget which team and I forget her name.

Joan had Bruce's leash looped around her wrist. I started talking non-stop. I started telling the girl about the summer before when Jennifer fell off her cousin's bicycle while riding down a hill. She had been pedalling backwards trying to apply the brakes but the bicycle was equipped with hand brakes which she had never seen before. She landed on the concrete sidewalk, on her chin, tearing open a cut as big as her mouth, breaking her jaw in three places and tearing out a couple of toenails. All she had been wearing was a pair of shorts. She had cuts and abrasions all over her body.

I held her hand in the hospital while an intern stitched up her chin and repaired her tiny toenails. I hate bragging about my kids but she was incredible. Not a whimper, not even when the intern was sewing up her chin or digging out the root of a toenail.

I kept telling the intern Jennifer's jaw was broken but he said that was impossible because she would be in so much pain she'd be screaming. But the lower part of her face looked a lot different so I knew it was broken.

I was so insistent the intern decided to x-ray the jaw, but he made it clear he was just doing it to humour me. And sure enough

120
The Lifeguard Springs into Action

there was a solid break under each ear and one in the chin area.

But by the time the x-rays were developed the intern had gone home and another presented me with the pictures. I suppose it would have been a little uncomfortable for the first one to have to face me.

I still have some notes Jennifer wrote to me after her jaw was wired shut.

'Daddy. I didn't fall off the bike. I jumped.'

'Why did you jump?' I asked her.

'Because it kept going faster and faster and I couldn't find the brakes.'

During the story, Bruce kept tugging at his leash. He wanted to go down to the edge of the water. I guess he was getting too hot. He finally took his chain in his mouth and tried to chew through it.

Joan couldn't be bothered getting up to take him down to the edge of the water so she just let go of the chain. Bruce trotted off towards the lake.

Moments later the lifeguard showed up.

'Sir, would you mind hanging on to your dog?'

I couldn't believe it. Where was he when my daughter was drowning? I was so mad I couldn't speak. Same with Joan.

'That's not a dog,' I blurted out, without knowing why.

'What is it then?' he said.

'It's my son. He's deformed.'

Then Joan went back to the van to make a pot of tea. I just sat there on the blanket with the kids. The Olympic swimmer rejoined her friends. I was questioning Alison about how she could have let Jennifer get out so far. Apparently Alison, who is three years older and that much taller, wanted to be up to her neck and Jennifer was trying to stay with her even though it was over her head.

But that all got settled. And all that time I found myself keeping my ears cocked for cries of help coming from the direction of the van. What if Joan were to get raped or mugged or something back there? I was on edge. I could imagine her crying out, 'Help! Rape!'

'Daddy?' said Jennifer. She was looking up from her *Mad*.

'Yes?'

'If I'd drowned would I have had my picture in the paper?'

The four of us went for a walk along the road. A workman in green denim was standing there holding a portable CB radio to his face.

He kept saying, '21 – Roger!' He was sweating.

A green truck loaded with workmen went by. Each workman had a long spike for picking up garbage. Each workman was being taken to his own special area of the beach.

Two of the workmen were Indians with long straight black hair and copper-coloured skin. They had sad faces. They were both wearing denim jackets in all that heat.

Other people kept going by in cars with their car radios blasting.

We got in the van and drove out of the park, back onto the US 5. Heading east into even further adventures.

121
The Natives of North America

We were now in New York State. We could see Lake Erie State Park on the left of the highway but the signs for the park said turn right so we did although it seemed strange. But the cut-off road curved off to the right and then switched back under an old stone tunnel under the highway. Through the tunnel you could see trees lining the road on the other side. It was a regular cloverleaf exit except that the exit was off a *two*-lane highway. I had a sense of déjà-vu about it. It must have been built in the early thirties. Maybe I'd seen a picture of it when I was a kid. Or – and this is always a possibility when you experience déjà-vus while travelling in the USA – maybe it had been in a movie and made strangely familiar that way although the movie itself had been long forgotten. As Gerry Gilbert says: 'Hands up those who have just had a déjà-vu.'

It's amazing how quickly even the best movies, the ones we enjoy the most, seep from our minds. So that when we see them a few years later it's as if we've never seen them before. That's especially true with such movies of the forties as *Casablanca* and *The Big Sleep*. Also *Young Man with a Horn* which I've seen once every three years since I was about ten years old. Books on the other hand stay with you. They require a greater expenditure of energy in order to experience them in the first place. And so they lock themselves in more firmly. Movies of the forties always remind me of my Uncle Ed who was shot by the Mafia in 1951. He was about twenty-three years old, about twelve years older than me. But we were strangely close. I was constantly modelling myself after him. He would always take me to see the latest Humphrey Bogart movie as it came out. I think it was my ninth birthday he bought me my very own trench coat and fedora. With my snub-nosed water pistol I could do a perfect imitation of Bogart saying, 'All right, sweetheart. Drop it!'

122
How to Become Part of Nature

But Lake Erie State Park was empty except for a human figure lying out in front of an old stone and wood house about four hundred feet away from the parking lot over an immense stretch of perfect green lawn.

We got out of the van and went over. There was a sign over the front door of the building. As we got closer we could read it. It said FIRST AID. It was the largest first aid station I'd ever seen. It looked more like a hospital. Actually it looked like an overgrown small-town railroad station.

The human figure was sleeping or lying quietly with his eyes closed. He was a park employee. He had a college zoology textbook by his side.

There were two giant change rooms inside the building. I went in the men's on the left. There were two showers on the south wall – no partitions, just showers. On the east wall was a row of coin-operated lockers. And on the north wall were two toilets, a washstand and a hot-air dryer. All this was dwarfed in the immensity of the room. There were marks on the floor where benches had been removed. The park had obviously been an enormously popular place at one time.

One of the toilets was badly messed up and stank. The other was clean and sweet-smelling but had no toilet paper. So I went in the smelly cubicle and took some toilet paper, then went into the clean one. When I pushed the hot-air dryer button water began shooting out of the spout and dripping down from the dryer itself. Someone had poured water into it. I was startled. I had been standing in a pool of water too. Lucky I hadn't been electrocuted. I thought with a shudder that Alison or Jennifer could have been killed instantly that way. Or any way. God, what would I do if something happened to either of them? I'd just fall apart like a swatted fly.

When I went back out the employee was sitting up reading his zoology textbook. I mentioned the water in the dryer. He didn't know what to do except let it dry out.

'Do you know anything about the history of this building?' I said, slapping my hand against the brick wall. 'Like for instance what it was before it was a change house?'

'This is my first summer working here,' he said. 'All I know is that it's been here since before I was born.'

I figured the second storey might be used for offices, and other rooms on the first floor for equipment. But I didn't bother asking him. I walked over to the top of the fifty-foot bluff overlooking the lake. There were some sailboats out there and a strong northeasterly wind was blowing cool. I sat on a bench and closed my eyes.

It was very relaxing. My personality disappeared and I became part of nature. The wind rocked my body as if I were a tree. It was such a pleasure not to be getting in the way of pure experience.

When I returned to the van Joan and the kids were making grilled cheese sandwiches. A gust of wind caught a plastic bag and sent it flying across the parking lot and into the trees. In Canada I might have chased it but I let it go because it was only the United States.

I looked at the map. If you drew a line due north from Lake Erie State Park it would run directly along Yonge Street in Toronto. Question: Is that interesting?

I dropped Joan and the kids off at a big department store in the little town of Wytheville. I wanted to get a haircut. But first I decided to take my watch into The Jewel Box, a little store on the main street. Moisture had been forming on the inside of the watch. You could see dewdrops inside the crystal.

123
The Jewel Box

The jeweller was a fat guy a few years younger than me. He was dressed as if he were running for mayor. He put down his Wall Street Journal and looked at the watch. 'I don't even think I know how to take it apart,' he said.

I should have walked out right there but instead, like a fool, I said, 'Oh go ahead, it's probably easier than it looks.'

He finally got the back off after much expenditure of energy. 'Oh look,' he said. 'Here's your trouble. The stem's broken off. That's how the moisture was getting in.'

He couldn't find another stem that would fit. He even took it down the street to another jeweller's then finally gave me back the watch in pieces.

'It's pretty unfortunate when your watch breaks down while you're travelling, I know,' he said. 'You don't know what to do. But there'll be no charge for that.'

A few days later, Frank, of Frank's Time Shop on Kenilworth Avenue in Hamilton, Ontario, said there was no way that stem was broken before the watch had been taken apart. 'Don't worry,' he said. 'That guy broke it for sure and was afraid to tell you.'

It was a really old-fashioned barber shop. Six chairs, no waiting. It was called the Wytheville Barber Shop.

My guy started cutting away. I almost fell asleep. He was talking about spring floods and all that kind of stuff. I started telling him a long-winded story about a barber who had a nervous break-

124
You Think It's Easy Being a Barber?

down as he was cutting my hair. He had to be taken away. 'The stress must have got to him', I said. I must have struck a chord for the guy started purring like a cat.

'Oh yes, it's a hard job, it really is', he said. 'People just laugh at you when you tell them but oh, it's a hard job all right.' He stopped and looked at himself in the mirror. He held his elbows out as if he were cutting my hair. 'It's hard holding your arms out like this all day', he said. 'It tightens your muscles right around the back. It's hard to get them untightened at the end of the day.'

I believed him totally. I hope I never have to be a barber. I'd rather be a bus-driver. Or maybe a watch repairman.

'Oh no', screamed Joan when we met fifteen minutes later. 'Your hair looks awful.'

I looked in the rear-view mirror. Sure enough, it was cut at all different lengths. It did look kind of stupid.

125
Nicodemus

We had to pay seventy-five cents to the parking lot attendant. He was a big fat guy in a neat uniform with white shirt and tie. His name was Nicodemus. He had a gun in a holster fastened to his belt.

'Hello there, Nicodemus', I said, handing him the money and my ticket. For some reason that did it: my friendly greeting combined with the Ontario licence plates. He wanted to talk. He wanted us to know he wasn't a native of Wytheville and as soon as he saved enough money he was moving back to his home town.

'Where's that?'

'Jacksonville, Florida', he said, proudly.

'You like it down there better than here?'

'It's the people', he said. 'The people are so much nicer down there. Not as many snobs.'

I asked him about his gun. Was it for shooting people who tried to crash through the gate without paying their seventy-five cents?

'No', he said. 'But a guard on a toll-gate on the highway was shot and killed for a quarter last week. He wouldn't let them go till they put in their money so they just shot him right between the eyes.'

But had he ever had to use his gun?

'Just once', he said. 'I'm not proud of this. It's not a very pleasant thing to have to tell and it's not a very pleasant thing to have to remember. I still sometimes lose sleep over it. I had to kill a man once.'

'What were the circumstances?'

'It was over in what we called Niggertown', he said, without apology although you could tell he knew it wasn't nice to call it Niggertown. 'I was night watchman at the warehouse and someone broke in. He drew a gun on me and so I shot him.'

126
The Monkey Man

Nicodemus stopped us just as we were about to pull away. 'Just a minute, sir. You've given me a Canadian quarter.'

'So what?'

'I haven't got anything against it. It's just that I got yelled at once for taking it so I don't take it anymore.'

I gave him another quarter. And I couldn't resist blasting off a bit. 'Jesus Christ', I said. 'For years when American money was worth a lot less than Canadian we always took silver at par anyway. It just wasn't considered worrying about unless it was over a dollar.'

'I know', he said, quietly.

As we pulled away the kids started screaming with delight. There was a man out in the road. He was jumping up and down like a monkey. He was dressed only in a pair of white jeans. He was just bounding up and down as if he had springs attached to his feet.

'Look at that man, Daddy. What's the matter with him?'

'That's a monkey man', I said, making it up as I went along. 'Most times they're just like you and me and every once in a while they just can't help it, they have to start acting like monkeys.'

The guy leaped up to a stoplight where a car was stopped. The people in the car were trying to get the windows rolled up. But it was too late. With one bounce, the monkey man jumped right through the back window. We just kept driving.

'Wow! Did you see that?' screamed the kids.

127
A Little Side Trip into the Mountains

As we drove further into New York State there was a gradual increase in the height of the bluffs along the shore. At times it looked like an eighty-foot sheer drop into the pounding surf of Lake Erie. There was a strong northeasterly wind.

To the southeast you could see the foothills of the Adirondacks. These are the hills you can see on a clear day from the north shore of Lake Erie around Featherstone Point.

'What are those mountains?' I used to ask my father.

'Those are the Blue Ridge Mountains of Pennsylvania,' he'd say.

Now it looked as if he'd been wrong. Those mountains over there were in New York State, not Pennsylvania.

But when I looked at the map I saw that yes my father was right after all. We were in New York State but the state line bends around to the south, and yes those mountains would be in Pennsylvania.

The mountains looked almost as far away from us as we drove along US 5 as they did when I was a kid standing on the beach on the Canadian side.

'Would you care to take a little side trip into the mountains?' I asked Joan.

'No. Some other time. I'm anxious to get home. I've got a lot to do before tomorrow.'

128
The Michelin Man

We stopped at a Sunoco station in Irving, New York. An enormously fat man covered in sweat came out. Grease was caked in all his creases.

There was an old Volkswagen van sitting there. It looked like the one Russell Seaworthy used to have, the one that he smashed up on the Skyway Bridge almost killing himself. The one that used to have the Michelin man sitting up on the roof, as if it were navigating. The Michelin man was sort of magic but it let him down that day on the Skyway Bridge when Russell was looking over at the skyline of Hamilton and ploughed into a slow-moving transport truck. Demolished the van and his teeth.

It seemed like a good idea to tell Russell about this one, especially if it were for sale. He loves the old-style vw vans but it's hard to find them in good condition.

'Is that van for sale?' I said.

'No, not really. It doesn't have a motor in it.'

'What year is it?'

'1966. Actually it does have a motor in it. It's got a big Chevy motor in it.' He looked at me and laughed. 'We're going to take it to the drags.'

'Have you raced it yet?'

'No. We took it out but it's too heavy for the van. We're going to have to change the wheels. We put the motor in the back. Maybe we should have put it in the front.'

The fat man waddled away in the summer heat, his arms sticking out horizontally like a barber. Imagine doing all that work just for the questionable fun of occasionally taking the van out on a quarter-mile track. Endless hours of toil, sweat, cursing. Then finding out you should have put the motor in the front. What a boring life!

Almost as bad as writing books. Writing a book then finding out you should have put the end at the beginning.

In front of modern motels in the US they have theatre-style marquees so they can put out any message they want and change it as often as they want.

Some of the older motels have signs reading FREE PHONE. Others say FREE PHONE AND TV.

More expensive motels say FREE PHONE AND TV IN EVERY ROOM.

Then there's COLOR TV IN EVERY ROOM.

A few years ago water beds were all the rage.

The latest thing is dirty movies, also known as skin flicks.

But you can't put up a sign outside a motel saying DIRTY MOVIES or SKIN FLICKS. It just doesn't sound right. So they put up signs saying ADULT MOVIES. Which kind of slanders the more intelligent breed of adult.

Some motels have signs saying ADULT MOVIES AND WATER BEDS.

I'd like to see a motel sign reading WILLING CHAMBERMAIDS or FREE STUD SERVICE.

It probably wouldn't do though for according to my pet theory most American males are impotent and most American females are frigid.

Somewhere in Ohio I thought I saw a sign reading SUNNYSIDE BROTHEL. But it went by so quickly I could be wrong.

AUTUMN REUNION NURSING HOME and SURFSIDE NURSING HOME are two signs worthy of mentioning.

'Oh look at that,' said Joan. 'How sick! Autumn Reunion Nursing Home.'

'Oh look, Daddy. Surfside Nursing Home,' said Alison. 'Does that mean the old people can go surfboard riding?' She was being cute.

'If you were an old woman in a nursing home wouldn't it be nice to be able to hear the surf?' I said.

'Yeah, I guess so,' said Alison.

As for the autumn reunion, I thought that was really poetic, not sick at all. I began dreaming of living in a nursing home reunited with all the boyfriends and girlfriends of my youth, all the beautiful boys and girls I've long lost touch with. That would be

129
Smug Complacency

absolutely sensational. Sometimes I just don't understand Joan. She's just too sophisticated for her own good.

I hated the motel sign reading IT JUST LOOKS EXPENSIVE. If that were true they could have just posted the rates on the sign.

But the worst sign of all was in front of a motel near Erie, Pennsylvania. It was the Capri Motel and it reminded me of all the smug complacency that political systems feed upon like grease. PRAY − BELIEVE − RECEIVE. That's what it said.

In other words, don't complain if you're not as rich as I am. It just means you haven't prayed as hard as I have or you haven't believed as deeply as I have.

That's probably the unspoken belief of the American establishment that runs the California vineyards, the Pentagon, and so forth, and refuses to put in an adequate medicare system.

130

Father Baker Bridge

There are huge steel mills on both sides of the Father Baker Bridge which leads into Buffalo from the south. The bridge is the same height as the smokestacks. Whichever way the wind is blowing the motorist and his passengers get lungs full of sulphur dioxide and poisonous particulate matter.

This is the end of Lake Erie, the rectum of a vast grey prehistoric animal which still groans in its sleep and dreams indecipherable dreams. This is where Lake Erie narrows into the Niagara River and through the billowing clouds of smoke we could see the faint outline of a Canadian woods far across the water.

'I can see Canada', I said.

'Where?' said the kids.

'Over there through the smoke.'

'Oh yeah', said Alison.

'I wish we were there now', said Jenny. 'Daddy?'

'Yes?'

'Do we have to go through the tunnel to get to Canada?'

'Do you want to?' I thought maybe the Detroit tunnel had frightened her.

'No', she said. 'You don't *see* anything in a tunnel.'

So. She *had* been frightened. 'No, Jenny. The tunnel was in *Detroit* at the other end of the lake.'

'Oh. What city is *this*?'

A guy in a yellow English sports car passed us. Then along came a guy in a black sports car and passed the yellow one.

'Buffalo.'

'Oh.'

And there at the entrance to the Peace Bridge, just after we paid our seventy-five cents, stood two hitchhikers. A man about twenty-eight who looked like the pop star David Bowie. And a girl standing in front of him, a little girl about Jenny's age, just coming up to his waist. A large thumb and a small thumb sticking out into the wind from onrushing cars.

Something about this apparition made my heart stop.

'Should we pick them up?'

'Yes, let's,' said Joan.

But we were in the outer lane and an impatient Cadillac with Ohio plates was nosing past us on our right. We were caught in traffic and couldn't stop, just as we had been in Detroit how many days earlier?

There was something magic and mysterious about these two hitchhikers, lonely, unreal, as if they were floating in the mist, about to disappear. My heart was aching for them. I wanted to know who they were and where they were going and I wanted to help them get there. I would have done anything for them.

That was July 5, 1977. About five in the afternoon. If you were about twenty-eight then, and looked like David Bowie, and were hitchhiking on the Peace Bridge into Canada with a nine-year-old girl, and if you happen to read these words somewhere, sometime, I don't care if it's forty years from now, please try to contact me. I'd sincerely love to hear from you.

In the middle of the Peace Bridge were three flags: the American flag, the United Nations flag, and the Canadian flag.

'We're in Canada,' I said as we passed the blue UN flag.

'Yay,' said the kids.

'Joan,' I said. 'I know this will sound crazy but I wouldn't mind turning around at the customs booth and going back and picking up those two hitchhikers.'

'They'd probably be picked up by now,' said Joan, sympathetically.

Anyway, the girl in the customs booth was nervous. It was as if she'd just started that day. Our car wasn't searched. She didn't find out about the geranium cutting we were smuggling across, the one Joan snitched from the park in Sandusky. By the way it has now grown quite a profusion of roots and is ready to be planted in Canadian soil.

133
Things Distinctively Canadian

We drove west along Highway 3 towards Port Colborne and Dunnville looking for things that were distinctively Canadian. That's what I like about the paintings of John Boyle. He just paints things that could only be found in Canada. It's not easy. Think about it.

'There's a maple leaf on the McDonald's sign,' said Alison. 'They don't have maple leaves on McDonald's signs in the States.'

'There's a car with Canadian licence plates,' said Jenny.

'There's a Dominion Store,' said Joan.

134
Mount Zion Cemetery

Since we were running along Highway 3 we decided to stop off at Mount Zion Cemetery where Joan's grandparents are buried. It's about three miles east of Dunnville.

I never knew Joan's grandfather. He died in 1956. His name was Charles Wilkins. He was a letter carrier. He loved fishing in the Grand River on his days off.

Joan says that just as Charlie was being lowered into his grave a huge fish jumped in the pond next to the cemetery. The cemetery was on a hill and you could see the pond easily. It was in a farmer's field. It was just a duck pond. You wouldn't think there'd be any fish in there.

When we pulled into Mount Zion Cemetery the first thing Joan said was, 'Oh, look! The pond's gone. All dried up.'

Joan's grandmother, Alice Wilkins, died in 1966. She was a tiny woman who even in old age was always aware of everything that was going on around her. She never withdrew from the moment. And now she was lying under the ground with Charlie.

Joan fixed up some of the plants growing around the tombstone and watered them.

I looked around. There was a fresh grave for a seventeen-year-old boy. A. Brett Cuthbertson 1960-1977.

There was a tombstone for a young man who had died at the age of twenty-two. His parents' names were also on the stone even though they were apparently still alive. Peter K. Schneider 1920-. His wife, Martha L. 1922- . Their son George L. 1952-1974.

There was one tombstone facing the wrong way. At least it was the only one in which the lettering faced west, towards the duck pond and the road. All the others faced east towards the rolling meadows and rising sun.

This tombstone facing the wrong way was fascinating. Orlan E. Neff. March 13 1920 – October 31 1949. Imagine dying on Hallowe'en 1949 in rural southern Ontario at the age of 29!

I wondered if Orlan E. Neff had ever driven all the way around

Lake Erie. I just felt he was a really funny character who died in some tremendously stupid accident. Ah, if only he could speak. If only you could put a quarter into a slot in the tombstone and listen to the shades wail and mumble. My mind was flooded with the possibilities of how Orlan E. Neff would sound.

Joan had to pee. She was trying to walk back to the car with her legs crossed. 'Let's go', she said.

'Why don't you just pee behind the tree?' I said. There was a 150-year-old maple tree right in the middle of the cemetery. And we were totally secluded.

'I couldn't pee in a cemetery', said Joan.

'Why not?' I said. I guess she was worried the dead people would be offended.

Joan didn't say anything but she looked thoughtful.

Meanwhile Bruce was running around peeing against tombstones left and right, marking out his territory. Saying BRUCE WAS HERE in the only language he knew. Urinese.

'Dogs pee in here all the time', I said.

That won her over, strangely enough. 'Okay', she said. She went behind the tree.

As she was peeing I slipped off my sandals and sneaked up behind her. I was just going to stick my head around the left side of the tree and say BOO!!! when Joan stuck her head around the right side of the tree and said BOO!!! I just about died.

135
It's Okay to Pee in a Cemetery

The cemetery reminded me a lot of the cemetery in one of my favourite movies: *The Night of the Living Dead.*

I lay down in the grass and remained perfectly still. I felt as if I were dead, lying there slowly disappearing along with all the other dead people. Along with all the dead fish, leaves, flowers, birds, worms, dogs and rabbits, rotting logs, mysterious memories, haunting thoughts, all dead and dying.

I figured in a thousand years there will be nothing left of us. Our forms will have been totally subsumed by other forms: new trees, new grass, new duck ponds, new people. The very atoms of our bodies might have dispersed all over the world hundreds of times, and might have temporarily constituted the bodies of dozens of human beings never mind other animals.

'Hey kids, why don't you lie down here with me and feel what it feels like to be dead?' It was like the voice of someone who wasn't there. It was like nothing talking.

136
The Night of the Living Dead

'Ech, no thanks', said Jennifer.

Alison just looked thoughtful. She knew she'd be dead some day. Might as well get used to it.

'Joan? Come and lie down.'

'No thanks.'

'Bruce?'

He stopped running around and cocked his ears.

137
Howard and Velma

'Let's drop in and see my mom and dad for a minute', said Joan. We were almost home. It was only a block out of our way. But still ...

'Aw, Joan, why don't we just go home first and then call them. You must be awfully tired.' Actually I was really anxious to see the house. I had a vague feeling something was wrong. It had burned to the ground in our absence or something like that.

'Okay', said Joan.

But then I began to feel guilty. I was the one who had told her not to buy that bathing suit in Painesville, Ohio, or wherever. I didn't want to rule her life with an iron fist. So when we came to the road leading to Joan's parents' place I turned.

Joan grabbed the wheel. 'No, it's okay, Dave. We'll just go home and phone them later.'

I turned anyway and we drove up their driveway. We could see them looking out from behind the living room drapes. We couldn't go home now.

Anyway, Howard and Velma were happy to see us. They wanted to know all about our trip. They particularly wanted to know how Alice and Charlie's grave looked.

'Joan peed in the cemetery', I said.

'Joan, you didn't', said Velma. Like mother, like daughter.

'Why you dirty squealer', said Joan.

138
A Moment in the Lives of Some White People

Howard was telling us about how the blacks are taking over the big American cities.

I told him we noticed in Detroit that the black neighbourhoods seemed a lot more upper class than the white.

'Ah, the poor whites', he said.

'The blacks are just as good as us', said Velma.

'They sure are', said Howard. 'If they can go through all the persecution they have and still rise to the top they must be as good as us. Some of them are real smart. They're starting to get educated.'

Howard wanted to know what big cities we'd gone through on our fabulous trip around Lake Erie.

'Detroit, Toledo, Cleveland, Erie and Buffalo.'

Howard and Velma are square dancers and have been on trips to square dancing conventions in places like Kansas City, Atlantic City and Los Angeles. We're always embarrassed by the large number of gifts they bring back for us. I have a Fonzie T-shirt from Kansas City and a GO BANANAS T-shirt from Atlantic City. The GO BANANAS T-shirt has a picture of a monkey sitting on the toilet and eating a banana. I wore it when I interviewed the Canadian folklorist Edith Fowke for *Quill and Quire*.

'We went over Cleveland when we went to Kansas City,' said Howard.

That didn't sound right. 'Are you sure?' I said.

'Oh no, I'm wrong. What made me think we'd gone over Cleveland was the pilot was a real card and when we were going over Chicago he announced that we should be passing over Chicago but it looked a lot like Cleveland.'

 139
Go Bananas

One down and four to go. Lakes that is.

We were telling Howard and Velma how we wanted to take trips around the four remaining Great Lakes now that we had been all the way around Lake Erie.

'You'll really like going around Lake Superior,' said Howard. 'I don't know about the American side but the Canadian side is real pretty.'

I said it would be fun going around Lake Michigan because it's the only one that is American on all sides.

Joan happens to have a friend who likes to go to Cape Cod and Joan is sort of interested in going there.

'When we go around Lake Michigan will we see Cape Cod?' she said.

'My God, what a lousy sense of geography you have,' I said. 'And you a school teacher!'

Everyone laughed. Joan prides herself on not having a sense of geography. It's an admirable quality. Not to know where you are geographically is the next best thing to nirvana.

140
Nirvana

When we pulled into our driveway our next-door neighbour, Audrey, came running out with a serious look on her face. She was wearing a David Bowie T-shirt.

'You better check your house right away,' she said. 'There's been

141
Dead Fish

an awful smell *comink* out of there all day.' Although born and raised in Anglo Canada Audrey always pronounced a hard *g* or almost a *k* sound on the end of her *ing* words. I've never drawn it to her attention, though I've been close to it at times, just out of curiosity, to see if she realizes it.

Sure enough there was an awful smell and it got worse as I approached the door.

When I opened the door there was an avalanche. I was buried in a huge heap of dead and rotting fish. The kind of fish that had been all over the beach at Point Pelee. The kind of fish Bruce had been rolling in and peeing on. The kind of fish I imagined decaying along with at the Mount Zion Cemetery.

For the next hour I shovelled dead fish out into the driveway and buried them in the backyard. The dead fish were in all the rooms. It was ghastly.

Worst of all, I couldn't figure out where all the fish had come from. It was almost as if God were angry, as if He didn't like white people to take trips all the way around one of His Great Lakes. It was His way of punishing us. I half-expected to uncover a pile of mouldy loaves of bread under the dead fish.

142

Business As Usual

After I finished shovelling out all the dead fish and burying them Joan and I started scrubbing the floors. We sent the kids over to Audrey's for the night. We threw out our rug. We sprayed Lysol everywhere. It was awful. We were really too busy to begin to discuss or to consider how the dead fish had got there.

Then when we finally had the place back in shape we were too exhausted to think about it.

I wearily checked the mail Audrey had been picking up for us. I had sent out a new book list just before we left and already the orders were starting to pour in. I was pleased.

I even had some orders from other poets which was sort of amazing because poets like to exchange books or get free review copies. They hardly ever buy books. This was most kind.

Ralph Gustafson had ordered a copy of *The Great Canadian Sonnet.*

Joe Rosenblatt had ordered a copy each of *Intense Pleasure* and *A Knight in Dried Plums.*

Dennis Lee had ordered a copy each of *The Saladmaker* and *Poems Worth Knowing.*

After my shower I was surprised when I checked our mileage book and discovered it all came out to even numbers. We had been gone one hundred hours and had travelled eight hundred miles.

Exactly. For an average of eight miles an hour. We'd spent $133.31.

As I flopped into bed I wondered how long it would take me to write *A Trip around Lake Erie.*

Would it take me less than one hundred hours? Probably. Would it earn me more than $133.31? Probably not.

Better still, would it be good?

And what lake would we go around next?

Typeset in Century Schoolbook and Helvetica Black
Printed in Canada at The Coach House Press
401 (rear) Huron Street, Toronto, Canada M5S 2G5

Photography: Montecolour
Text Design: Glenn Goluska